An Analysis of

Roland Barthes's

The Death
of the Author

Laura Seymour

Published by Macat International Ltd
24:13 Coda Centre, 189 Munster Road, London SW6 6AW.

Distributed exclusively by Routledge
2 Park Square, Milton Park, Abingdon, Oxon OX14 4RN
711 Third Avenue, New York, NY 10017, USA

Routledge is an imprint of the Taylor & Francis Group, an informa business

www.macat.com
info@macat.com

Cataloguing in Publication Data
A catalogue record for this book is available from the British Library.
Library of Congress Cataloguing-in-Publication Data is available upon request.
Cover illustration: Angus Greig

ISBN 978-1-912453-51-1 (hardback)
ISBN 978-1-912453-06-1 (paperback)
ISBN 978-1-912453-21-4 (e-book)

Notice
The information in this book is designed to orientate readers of the work under analysis,
to elucidate and contextualise its key ideas and themes, and to aid in the development
of critical thinking skills. It is not meant to be used, nor should it be used, as a
substitute for original thinking or in place of original writing or research. References and
notes are provided for informational purposes and their presence does not constitute
endorsement of the information or opinions therein. This book is presented solely for
educational purposes. It is sold on the understanding that the publisher is not engaged
to provide any scholarly advice. The publisher has made every effort to ensure that
this book is accurate and up-to-date, but makes no warranties or representations with
regard to the completeness or reliability of the information it contains. The information
and the opinions provided herein are not guaranteed or warranted to produce particular
results and may not be suitable for students of every ability. The publisher shall not be
liable for any loss, damage or disruption arising from any errors or omissions, or from
the use of this book, including, but not limited to, special, incidental, consequential or
other damages caused, or alleged to have been caused, directly or indirectly, by the
information contained within.

CONTENTS

THE MACAT LIBRARY

The Macat Library is a series of unique academic explorations of seminal works in the humanities and social sciences – books and papers that have had a significant and widely recognised impact on their disciplines. It has been created to serve as much more than just a summary of what lies between the covers of a great book. It illuminates and explores the influences on, ideas of, and impact of that book. Our goal is to offer a learning resource that encourages critical thinking and fosters a better, deeper understanding of important ideas.

Each publication is divided into three Sections: Influences, Ideas, and Impact. Each Section has four Modules. These explore every important facet of the work, and the responses to it.

This Section-Module structure makes a Macat Library book easy to use, but it has another important feature. Because each Macat book is written to the same format, it is possible (and encouraged!) to cross-reference multiple Macat books along the same lines of inquiry or research. This allows the reader to open up interesting interdisciplinary pathways.

To further aid your reading, lists of glossary terms and people mentioned are included at the end of this book (these are indicated by an asterisk [*] throughout) – as well as a list of works cited.

Macat has worked with the University of Cambridge to identify the elements of critical thinking and understand the ways in which six different skills combine to enable effective thinking.
Three allow us to fully understand a problem; three more give us the tools to solve it. Together, these six skills make up the **PACIER** model of critical thinking. They are:

ANALYSIS – understanding how an argument is built
EVALUATION – exploring the strengths and weaknesses of an argument
INTERPRETATION – understanding issues of meaning

CREATIVE THINKING – coming up with new ideas and fresh connections
PROBLEM-SOLVING – producing strong solutions
REASONING – creating strong arguments

To find out more, visit **WWW.MACAT.COM.**

CRITICAL THINKING AND "THE DEATH OF THE AUTHOR"

Primary critical thinking skill: INTERPRETATION
Secondary critical thinking skill: CREATIVE THINKING

Reading "The Death of the Author" provides us with new critical thinking skills for interpreting all kinds of texts, including literary texts. Most specifically, Roland Barthes's work is concerned with where a text's meaning lies. Rather than directing our interpretations of a text toward fixed ideas about the author's intended meaning, he argues that the potentially infinite readers of a text can generate equally infinite interpretations of that text.

Barthes thinks creatively about the question of the author's authority. He deploys new terms and uses language in creative ways to convey his new ideas. The key new term Barthes uses is "scriptor." He aims for the idea of the scriptor (which neutrally represents the act of writing as devoid of authorial intentionality) to replace the traditional notion of the author.

ABOUT THE AUTHOR OF THE ORIGINAL WORK

Roland Barthes was born in Cherbourg, Manche, in north-west France in 1915. His father, Luis Barthes, was a navy officer who died in 1916 when the fishing vessel he commanded was attacked by a flotilla of German destroyers. Barthes was raised by his mother, Henriette Barthes (née Binger). His secondary education took place in Paris at the Lycée Montaigne, and then at the Lycée Louis-Grand. He then moved on to study classics, grammar, and philology at the Sorbonne. Barthes became an educator himself, teaching at several lycées and tertiary educational establishments before ending up as a Chair at the Collège de France. Barthes died in 1980 from injuries sustained when he was hit by a van while walking through Paris. Barthes has a reputation as a philosopher and writer who was very influential in structuralism and post-structuralism.

ABOUT THE AUTHOR OF THE ANALYSIS

Laura Seymour has a BA in English Literature, an M.Phil in Renaissance Literature, and a PhD in Shakespeare Studies. She has published various book chapters on cognition and early modern literature. She is not affiliated with any institution.

ABOUT MACAT

GREAT WORKS FOR CRITICAL THINKING

Macat is focused on making the ideas of the world's great thinkers accessible and comprehensible to everybody, everywhere, in ways that promote the development of enhanced critical thinking skills.

It works with leading academics from the world's top universities to produce new analyses that focus on the ideas and the impact of the most influential works ever written across a wide variety of academic disciplines. Each of the works that sit at the heart of its growing library is an enduring example of great thinking. But by setting them in context – and looking at the influences that shaped their authors, as well as the responses they provoked – Macat encourages readers to look at these classics and game-changers with fresh eyes. Readers learn to think, engage and challenge their ideas, rather than simply accepting them.

'Macat offers an amazing first-of-its-kind tool for interdisciplinary learning and research. Its focus on works that transformed their disciplines and its rigorous approach, drawing on the world's leading experts and educational institutions, opens up a world-class education to anyone.'

Andreas Schleicher
Director for Education and Skills, Organisation for Economic Co-operation and Development

'Macat is taking on some of the major challenges in university education … They have drawn together a strong team of active academics who are producing teaching materials that are novel in the breadth of their approach.'

Prof Lord Broers,
former Vice-Chancellor of the University of Cambridge

'The Macat vision is exceptionally exciting. It focuses upon new modes of learning which analyse and explain seminal texts which have profoundly influenced world thinking and so social and economic development. It promotes the kind of critical thinking which is essential for any society and economy. This is the learning of the future.'

Rt Hon Charles Clarke, former UK Secretary of State for Education

'The Macat analyses provide immediate access to the critical conversation surrounding the books that have shaped their respective discipline, which will make them an invaluable resource to all of those, students and teachers, working in the field.'

Professor William Tronzo, University of California at San Diego

WAYS IN TO THE TEXT

KEY POINTS

- Roland Barthes was a French philosopher and linguist most noted for his work on the structures of texts.
- "The Death of the Author" is about whether the flesh and blood author of a text should be considered important.
- This book is distinctive as one of the key works of structuralism.

Who Was Roland Barthes?

Roland Barthes was born in Cherbourg, Manche, in north-west France. His father, Luis Barthes, was a navy officer who died in battle in 1916. Barthes was raised by his mother, Henriette Barthes (née Binger). His secondary education took place in Paris at the Lycée* Montaigne followed by the Lycée Louis-Grand. He then moved on to study classics, grammar, and philology at the Sorbonne. Barthes became an educator himself, teaching at several lycées and tertiary educational establishments before ending up as a Chair at the Collège de France. Barthes died in 1980 from injuries sustained when he was hit by a van while walking through Paris.

Barthes wrote "The Death of the Author" while he was the Director of Studies at École Practique des Hautes Études in Paris. He was always interested in moving between academia and popular culture. This is reflected by the fact that "The Death of the Author" was first published alongside works of pop culture. Richard Howard* first published it, translated to English, in a 1967 issue of *Aspen,** an American cultural journal. *Aspen* included art; music, e.g. lyrics by John Lennon, a member of the English pop group, *The Beatles*; creative writing, such as work by English novelist J.G. Ballard; and works of literary and cultural criticism, such as "The Death of the Author." Publication in *Aspen* highlights Barthes's interest in all aspects of popular culture, from film and music to advertising. The fact that "The Death of the Author" was first published in English demonstrates Barthes's international outlook as a writer and academic. Later, in 1968, the original French text was published in the French journal *Manteia.** The latest translation of the text, which was done by Stephen Heath* and appears in the 1977 edition of the Barthes anthology *Image – Music – Text*, is considered standard.

Barthes has a reputation as a philosopher and writer who was very influential in structuralism* and post-structuralism.*

What Does "The Death of the Author" Say?
In "The Death of the Author," Barthes argues that we should stop seeing the "real person" who wrote a book as important. He suggests that we ought not to interpret a book by referring to the author's biography. What an author believed (or is said to have believed) is not important to the understanding of his or her book. The author's own comments about the book itself are equally unimportant. The title "The Death of the Author" can also allude to the following difference between an author and a text: an author can die, but the text they have written can remain after them and still be understood.

The flesh and blood author of a text may or may not actually be physically dead, this is not the "death" to which Barthes is referring. For Barthes, authors are always "dead" in the sense that they are not significant and do not control the text we are reading, or the reading process.

This conclusion is important because it provides us with new options for reading a text. Our readings of texts—whether they are literary texts or historical documents—no longer need to be trammeled by considerations regarding the person who wrote them. Instead, we can feel freer as readers to interpret a text simply on its own merits. One example involves considering an author's gender. If we follow Barthes's ideas, we may decide we do not need to know an author's gender in order to interpret the meaning of their words. Whether or not you agree with Barthes, "The Death of the Author" is significant because it prompts us to think about how we consider the relationships between authors and texts. It leads us to consider questions such as: why might an author be considered a more authoritative reader of their text than any other type of reader? And which aspects of an author's life do we consider to be more materially related to the interpretation of their texts than others?

"The Death of the Author" has had a huge impact on literary theory. Its popularity is made clear simply by the prevalence of its translations. Originally written in French, it has been published in numerous different languages including English, Spanish, Japanese, and Dutch.

Why Does "The Death of the Author" Matter?

Reading "The Death of the Author" is a good way to think more critically about how we perform literary analyses. More specifically, it prompts us to evaluate when and why we bring information about an author's life and personality to bear on our understanding of their texts. It also prompts us to question the usefulness of doing so. Barthes's theories can be applied to all kinds of texts in addition to literary ones (e.g. scripts for TV shows, politicians' speeches, legal documents, and even letters or text messages between friends). Almost all jobs and academic disciplines involve reading and understanding texts, so the critical thinking stimulated by reading "The Death of the Author" can be applied very broadly in our lives.

Though several critical theories about readers, authors, and texts exist, "The Death of the Author" contains some unique and original ideas which set it apart. Barthes's replacement of the traditional term "author" with "the scriptor" is one example of such an idea. Barthes's abstract notion of "the reader" is also different from many other reader-response theorists. Many reader-response theorists, when they talk of readers, mean real readers of flesh and blood. For Barthes, however, "the reader" simply means the conceptual space where all the many potential meanings of a text are contained.

This essay is also important beyond the immediate context of the academic classroom because it prompts us to think about our human relationships to writing and meaning. Humanity continues to create texts and to examine systems of signs—from music to the Highway Code*—for meaning, often looking to authorial intention for the source of that meaning. Our enduring need to communicate with one another ensures that theories and critiques of language, text, and significance will always be needed. In addition, many authors today continue to be worldwide celebrities not only because of the quality of their writing, but also because of who they are as people. For many readers, the link between a flesh and blood author and his or her texts remains strong. Critiquing the significance of this link becomes a useful way of understanding present day literary culture. As such, "The Death of the Author" remains important to us today and certainly has the potential to continue to be important in years to come.

SECTION 1
INFLUENCES

MODULE 1
THE AUTHOR AND THE HISTORICAL CONTEXT

KEY POINTS

- "The Death of the Author" is a significant work that helps us to rethink the relationships between readers, authors, and texts.

- Roland Barthes was a philosopher and linguist with an interest in popular culture.

- "The Death of the Author" was written at a time of radical upheaval in Paris.

Why Read This Text?

"The Death of the Author" is an important work to read because it provides a critique of the relationships between readers, authors, and texts. Many readers, without really thinking about it, will use information about the author's life and (perceived) personality to inform their interpretation of that author's texts. This information might include details about the author's gender, friendship circle, and any events—whether traumatic or happy—that befell them. Roland Barthes asks us to examine what our readings of texts would be like if we ceased doing this. He asks us to consider the author as figuratively "dead" to us and lacking any authority over their text. Information about the author becomes irrelevant to our reading of his or her texts.

Another reason to read "The Death of the Author" is because it has been a highly influential book, both within structuralism and beyond. Though Barthes's theories, as expressed in this work, are often applied to our interpretations of literary texts, they can be applied to any texts. Thus, "The Death of the Author" can help us critique how we

> **66** To give writing its future, it is necessary to overthrow the myth: the birth of the reader must be at the cost of the death of the Author. **99**
>
> Roland Barthes, "The Death of the Author"

understand authorship in other academic disciplines. For instance, if we are studying legal texts we might use this work to question the relationship of those texts to their authors. Barthes's theories can also apply to our everyday lives and to popular culture. For instance, we can apply them as we read pop culture texts such as celebrity interviews. These theories will also be useful for grappling with questions of authority. For example, when analyzing a person's will it is crucial to know if any changes to that will were done with their consent and were thus "authored" by them.

Author's Life

Relating Barthes's life to "The Death of the Author" would be, ironically, to read the text precisely how he asks us not to. Though Barthes argues that details about an author are irrelevant for understanding their texts, certain details of Barthes's life suggest that "The Death of the Author" could only have been written by him, at a particular place and time.

Barthes spent relatively long periods alone in sanatoria, suffering from tuberculosis. Thus, until the mid-1940s, much of his post-doctoral thinking was not overly influenced by the doctrines of a particular institution. Being so far removed from academia meant Barthes was a thinker outside the limitations of institutional schools and able to critique the ways in which the academics in these institutions thought and wrote. Some critics have suggested that Barthes's homosexuality was also important because it prompted him to critique the flaws of entrenched heteronormative* ways of thinking.

Barthes was not a total outsider to academic circles. At the time he wrote "The Death of the Author," Barthes was Director at the École Prâctique des Hautes Études in Paris, where he had studied classics, grammar, and philology (taking significant periods of time away to recuperate from his illness). Structuralism was well established at the Sorbonne, and Barthes was part of this movement. He taught and researched in semiology,* and produced a book on this topic, the structuralist *Elements of Semiology* (1964). Many critics agree that "The Death of the Author" marks the beginning of Barthes's critique of structuralism. In 1966, Barthes attended a significant seminar on structuralism at Johns Hopkins University* alongside Jacques Derrida,* who was also engaged in a critique of the movement.

How far Barthes's family life impacted his thoughts is open to interpretation. A psychoanalytic reading might see the death of Barthes's father nearly a year after he was born as relevant to his theory of the dead or insignificant author. Like the father in psychoanalytic theories of the Oedipus complex,* the author was a godlike figure to whom Barthes denied significance and sought to "kill off." Some critics and biographers have put forward such theories, noting that Barthes said of his father's death that he had "no father to kill, no family to hate, no milieu to reject: great Oedipal frustration!"[1] However, these readings are often contested or discounted.

Author's Background

Barthes's "The Death of the Author" was written and published in an era of French history dominated by a particular instance of radicalism: the civic unrest of 1968. Early in May 1968, students from Paris's schools and universities protested Charles de Gaulle's* conservative government by occupying buildings and a series of workers' strikes followed. The police were deployed to end the protests by arresting students, resulting in violence in the streets as students resisted. The unrest spilled into June with ongoing strikes lasting between five and six weeks before the government finally regained control. The protesters' aim, which ultimately failed, was to oust de Gaulle from government. May 1968 inspired other such protests across the globe: in Europe (notably Germany and Italy), Japan, South America, and the United States. Often these protests were combined with anger at the Vietnam War. Barthes's radical notion of the death of the author could be linked with this general climate of radicalism.

The 1960s was also a period dominated by the Cold War (1947–1991).* This tension between the US and its NATO* allies (the "Western Bloc") and the USSR* and its allies (the "Eastern Bloc") affected academics at the time in many ways. France was one of the US's allies during the Cold War and had begun its own nuclear program under de Gaulle just after the end of World War II. The first French nuclear test took place in 1960. Present day readers of Barthes's work might investigate the fact that "The Death of the Author" was very quickly translated into English and published in the US against the backdrop of the Cold War. This might suggest that many academic alliances were forged along the same channels as political alliances at the time.

NOTES

1   See for instance Roland Barthes, *Roland Barthes*, trans. Richard Howard (New York: Farrar, Straus and Giroux, 1977), 45.

ACADEMIC CONTEXT

KEY POINTS

- "The Death of the Author" was written at a high point of structuralism, but also at a time when structuralism was being challenged.

- Jacques Derrida, Claude Lévi-Strauss,* and Ferdinand de Saussure* were key players in Roland Barthes's field.

- Jacques Derrida, Julia Kristeva,* and Honoré de Balzac* are some of the main figures with whom Barthes engaged in his work.

The Work in its Context

"The Death of the Author" was written during a high point of structuralism, but also at a time when structuralism was beginning to be challenged. "The Death of the Author" itself can be read as one of those challenges.

Structuralism was a theoretical movement beginning in the early twentieth century that spanned several disciplines such as literary studies, linguistics, and anthropology. Structuralism as a movement emphasizes how any single phenomenon can only be understood as part of a wider system or pattern. Structuralism was well established in continental Europe by the mid-twentieth century. However, in the 1960s, a number of thinkers, later called "post-structuralists,"* began to make changes in the theory. Post-structuralists criticized structuralism's idea that such a stable, coherent system of meaning exists at all. They focused instead on the relativity *within* systems and the gaps existing within the logic of the system. Another critique of structuralism was the practice of deconstruction,* which questioned

> ❝ Man does not exist prior to language, either as a
> species or as an individual. ❞
> Roland Barthes, "The Death of the Author"

the hierarchies, coherences, and claims to unity of the structuralist system. In 1967, the same year "The Death of the Author" was first published, Jacques Derrida published what are often seen as the seminal works of deconstruction: *Of Grammatology* and *Writing and Difference*.

Overview of the Field

"The Death of the Author" marks a turn in Roland Barthes's thoughts from structuralism toward post-structuralism.

Structuralism was a school of thought that straddled and connected several disciplines, including literature, linguistics, and anthropology. The structural linguistics of Ferdinand de Saussure is based on the idea that words do not have meanings when taken by themselves. It is only within the wider system of language that words have meaning. Saussure called this system of language *langue* and the individual use of a single word *parole*. The structural anthropology of Claude Lévi-Strauss suggested that human societies make meaning by dividing the world up into systems of binary opposites, for example: raw food vs cooked food or male vs female.

Post-structuralism was beginning to challenge the entrenched environment of structuralism during Barthes's intellectual lifetime. Post-structuralists questioned the stability of the systems that had been posited by structuralists. Simultaneously, deconstruction was also posing, as it continues to pose, a challenge to structuralist ways of thinking. The philosopher Jacques Derrida, whose name is often thought of as synonymous with deconstruction, argued that, above and beyond the death of the author, texts cannot be said to have any point of "origin" at all. They are, as he says, "without center."[1] Derrida denied that some aspects of a text might be more authoritative than others. This is seen starkly in his essay "Parergon" (1978), which elevates the frame around a work of art to a status level parallel with the work of art itself. Derrida describes the Parergon as "the supplement outside the work," such as a painting's frame, and yet he argues that something supplementary can still have a subversive power.[2]

Academic Influences

"The Death of the Author" is informed by a combination of Barthes's own original thought and his engagement with other academics, such as Jacques Derrida. Barthes had many close friendships with intellectuals which involved exchanges of ideas. One notable friendship was with his student Julia Kristeva who used the techniques of psychoanalysis* to challenge structuralist ideas, focusing instead on what is absent or repressed in the structuralist system.

In addition to being open about how he was influenced by writers such as Derrida and Kristeva, Barthes was also influenced by his readings of literary texts. He was drawn to particular authors, even though he discounts the importance of the author to literary interpretation. Barthes mentions several intertextual* influences in "The Death of the Author," for example, the French writer Honoré de Balzac (in particular Balzac's story Sarrasine, which Barthes also analyses in his 1970 book S/Z), the French novelist Marcel Proust,* the Dutch painter Vincent Van Gogh,* and the French poet Charles Baudelaire.* These, and the other people Barthes mentions, were known as famous figures with interesting personalities. Though he invokes these notable cultural icons, in "The Death of the Author" Barthes denies that the personalities and interesting lives of writers and artists like them are a significant influence on how their works are read and understood. He describes the fame of these authors only to emphasize that this fame belongs to them as people and should not influence the way in which we read their texts. "The Death of the Author" was well received, and was quickly absorbed into the thought patterns of post-structuralists, such as Michel Foucault* in his 1969 essay "What is an Author?" which also sought to deny privileged status to the flesh and blood author of a text.

NOTES

1   Jacques Derrida, *Writing and Difference*, translated by Alan Bass (London: Routledge & Kegan Paul, 1978) p. 353.

2   Jacques Derrida, 'Parergon', in *The Truth in Painting*, translated by Geoff Bennington and Ian McLeod (Chicago: Chicago University Press, 1978), p. 55.

MODULE 3
THE PROBLEM

KEY POINTS

- Roland Barthes was asking some key questions: what is an author, and how might authors be unimportant for understanding texts?

- Psychoanalysis, Deconstruction, the New Criticism* movement, and The Cambridge School* were all important participants in this debate.

- Barthes was in conversation with many of the main participants in the debate.

Core Question

The intellectual battlefield significant at the time Roland Barthes was writing "The Death of the Author" centered on the issue of subjectivity, particularly authorial subjectivity. Established humanist* and Romantic* notions of the human subject stressed the importance of authors as individuals, and lauded the traits of autonomy,* personality, or genius. This emphasis on personality presumed that the authors' biographies and individual traits (including, as Barthes stressed in his critique of this view, their destructive personality traits) were of primary importance to understanding a text because they provided insight into the intention of the writing. Marxist* theorists added the notion of the author as a capitalist* "owner" or proprietor of their texts who controls their use and consumption by limiting the ways in which they can be interpreted. In "The Death of the Author," Barthes was, like several of his contemporaries, reacting against the validation of the author as a great personality and/or a capitalist owner constraining the interpretation of a text.

> **❝** Though the sway of the Author remains powerful (the new criticism has often done no more than consolidate it), it goes without saying that certain writers have long since attempted to loosen it. **❞**
> Roland Barthes, "The Death of the Author"

In England and America, two critical movements were also working to dismantle this Romantic ideal: the Cambridge School of literary criticism and the New Criticism movement, both of which began in the early twentieth century. According to New Criticism, texts must be read without considering any form of external context (be that the context provided by the text's author, by history, or by the readership). The French brand of New Criticism was called *la nouvelle critique*. Unlike New Criticism, *la nouvelle critique* was often grounded in the importance of the reader as an interpreter of texts. *La nouvelle critique* was seen to be important because it liberated readers from having to interpret texts according to authorial intention alone.

The Participants

The New Critics W.K. Wimsatt* and Monroe Beardsley* published a 1946 essay called "The Intentional Fallacy"* (based on a 1939 essay they had written on "Intention"), contending that a text's meaning is not constrained by the author or authorial intention. Wimsatt and Beardsley emphasized that we can only partially reconstruct the author's intention from a text, and we can never say with certainty what the author intended. Marxist critics such as the French writer Pierre Macherey* were meanwhile attacking the idea of the author as a form of capitalist proprietor or owner of a text. Many members of the broader intellectual community reacted strongly against these ideas, seeing them as too radical, difficult to understand, and disrespectful of tradition.

Thus, deconstruction, post-structuralism, New Criticism, and the Cambridge School had their opponents. One opponent, the French literary critic and Sorbonne professor Raymond Picard,* took issue with Barthes in particular in his 1964 essay *New Criticism or New Fraud? (Nouvelle Critique ou Nouvelle Imposture?)*. He argued that understanding a text's historical and autobiographical context was crucial for understanding the text itself.

Several other post-structuralist theorists produced related works at the time. For example, Michel Foucault's "What is an Author?" (1969) also relegated the author to being simply a function of language rather than the creator of language. Foucault argued that the real physical author of a text should not be thought to be constraining that text's meaning. Authors of related works, such as Foucault, tended to receive Barthes's ideas well at that time.

The Contemporary Debate

Barthes can be considered to be writing alongside certain authors, and to be engaging directly in conversations, or igniting debates, with others.

"The Death of the Author" fitted in with contemporary anti-capitalist critiques of the bourgeois cult of the author, such as Pierre Macherey's Marxist discussion in his book *A Theory of Literary Production* (1966). Macherey argued that a text is, by virtue of being read, no longer neatly contained by its author but "consumed" and made "to move out from the provisional container of the book into the minds of possible readers."[1] Barthes was also considered one of the main proponents of *la nouvelle critique*, which means his work is considered alongside other thinkers in this school of thought such as Georges Poulet.*

Barthes was directly in conversation with other thinkers, notably Michel Foucault and his one-time pupil, the celebrated feminist philosopher and psychoanalyst, Julia Kristeva. Kristeva critically blended Barthes's work with psychoanalytic thought.

With some other writers, Barthes' work began an angry debate more than a conversation. "The Death of the Author" met with negative reception from many more traditional theorists who believed that the author was highly significant. In his 1964 tract *New Criticism or New Fraud? (Nouvelle Critique ou Nouvelle Imposture?)*, Raymond Picard attacked New Critics, focusing specifically on Barthes. Picard argued that New Criticism hypocritically made great claims to generating new and more accurate understandings of literary texts, but that these claims simply could not work in practice. Deploying Freudian* theory, Picard contended that this was because an author's text is intimately bound up with that author's life. Therefore, Picard argued, the idea of the death of the author stops texts from being interpreted properly.

NOTES

1   Pierre Macherey, *A Theory of Literary Production*, trans. Geoffrey Wall (London: Routledge, 2006), 15.

MODULE 4
THE AUTHOR'S CONTRIBUTION

KEY POINTS

- Roland Barthes wanted to replace the idea of "the author" with that of "the scriptor."

- Breaking away from his previous structuralist approach, Barthes started to question the axioms of structuralism.

- Barthes adapted the current New Critical idea of the reader, suggesting that the reader is also a depersonalized phenomenon.

Author's Aims

Roland Barthes's objective in "The Death of the Author" is to convince readers that the intentions, subjectivity, and biography of an author ought not, and cannot, be used to interpret his or her text. Additionally, he argues that, because there is no appreciable authorial intention to give a text a *single* meaning, texts do not have a stable, unitary meaning. Rather, texts are what he calls a "composite" of different interpretations provided by readers.[1]

He mounts a challenge to orthodoxy by calling on readers to throw aside the traditional post-Enlightenment* idea of the overriding significance of the author. Barthes distinguishes his approach from other members of the New Criticism school with which he was associated. He argues that, though they purport to read texts as autonomous entities, many New Critics actually perpetuate the idea of the author as fundamental to a text's meaning.

Barthes modified the ideas of New Critics slightly in other ways, further marking out his different approach. Like many New Critics, he postulated that the reader was very important. However, by "the

> 66 The hand, cut off from any voice, borne by a pure gesture of inscription. 99
>
> Roland Barthes, "The Death of the Author"

reader" he did not mean (as many New Critics did) a particular physical person but an abstract conceptual space where all possible meanings of a text are contained. Barthes does not only argue that the author should not be thought of as a person of flesh and blood, the reader also becomes more abstract. It may be argued that one key consequence of this abstraction is that learned readers cannot set themselves up as authorities in place of the author.

Approach

In "The Death of the Author," Barthes frames the question of authorship as a question of authority. This makes sense, as the word "author" has etymological links to the Latin word "auctoritas" which means the power to command or to establish. Barthes's approach involves linking the author's authority over a text to numerous other types of authority, including the divine. Barthes's approach to the question of authorship is thus a very iconoclastic* one. It also sees the "authority" of authors as part of a wider problem about who we allow to command us and to determine our interpretation of the world.

Barthes argues that we should redefine the way we read literary texts, aiming not to "decipher" them (i.e. to provide a univocal explanation), but rather to "detangle" their numerous possible readings.[2] One intended effect of this approach is to destabilize the power of the literary critic, who had aimed to act as the mouthpiece of the author and explain the single authoritative meaning of the text. In "The Death of the Author," Barthes presents such critics as pugnaciously seeking "victory for the Critic" and assuming a role that gives them power to govern other readers' understandings of the text.[3] His approach is to dismantle that role.

Barthes demonstrates his new approach through a reading of literary texts by authors such as Proust and Balzac, and by discussing the relationships between these writers' lives and their work. When it comes to Proust, Barthes makes the astounding claim that Proust's work did not imitate his life and times. Rather, Proust's life and times imitated his work. This claim is perhaps deliberately provocative. It seems surreal to think the people, texts, and objects in the century when Proust lived were arranging themselves to resemble his work. Barthes may have been making this statement to emphasize how minutely and prophetically realistic Proust's works were. We might compare this to today's phenomenon of influential TV shows and films which result in everyday people attempting to talk, dress, and act like their favorite characters.

Contribution in Context

Barthes arrived at his key concept of the death of the author through a sustained examination of the ways in which texts generate and transmit meaning. His thoughts were influenced by other structuralist and post-structuralist thinkers, and by mid-twentieth century challenges to what was known as "the intentional fallacy." The intentional fallacy is the idea that authorial intention is both recoverable from a text and the locus of that text's meaning.

Barthes's ideas and themes situate him firmly alongside thinkers who attacked the intentional fallacy. However, not all previous writers who had challenged the intentional fallacy then moved on, like Barthes, to emphasize the importance of the reader. For members of the Cambridge School of criticism such as F.R. Leavis* and William Empson,* both authorial intention and readers' interpretations were discounted as external to the meaning of a text. On the other hand, another of Barthes's contemporaries, the French Marxist theorist

Pierre Macherey, conceptualized the problem in terms of the relative importance of author and reader. He contended that readers were more important than authors.[4]

"The Death of the Author" emerged from both literary and political contexts. It was shaped by debates about the literary author and by Marxism's challenge to entrenched ideas of ownership and property (which generates questions about who is the owner of a text). The idea of the death, or insignificance, of the author was also being articulated by other influential thinkers such as Michel Foucault and Jacques Derrida.

NOTES

1   Roland Barthes, "The Death of the Author," in *Image – Music – Text*, trans. Stephen Heath (New York: Hill and Wang, 1977), 142.

2   Barthes, "The Death of the Author."

3   Barthes, "The Death of the Author."

4   Pierre Machery, *Theory of Literary Production* (London: Routledge, 2006).

SECTION 2
IDEAS

MODULE 5
MAIN IDEAS

KEY POINTS

- Roland Barthes argues that authors should be disregarded when we try to understand texts.
- He replaces the traditional idea of the author with the more neutral idea of the scriptor.
- Barthes describes the scriptor as a kind of disembodied hand.

Key Themes

The main theme of Roland Barthes's "The Death of the Author" is the idea that authors, however great and interesting their personal lives, should be disregarded when we try to understand texts. Another main theme is that of the importance of the reader. For Barthes in "The Death of the Author," the reader has an important role in determining what a text means. A third key theme of the essay is the notion that a text, rather than being unified by a single meaning, interpretation, or aim, is a meeting-point, even a clash, of several discourses and interpretations.

Barthes begins by stating his key claim: that authors are separate from their texts, and thus that we can never discover the meaning of a text by reference to the author. He then discusses the "fiction" of the author as a single person who governs a text's meaning and gives examples of famous authors and their relationships to their texts.

Next, Barthes focuses on the importance of the text compared to the author. He argues that we should not interpret texts by referencing their authors. Instead, we should look at the text as an autonomous entity, examining the many meanings that readers can find within it.

> 66 The removal of the Author ... is not merely an historical fact or an act of writing; it utterly transforms the modern text. 99
>
> Roland Barthes, "The Death of the Author"

The final sentence of the essay is the culmination of Barthes's argument. It states, "The birth of the reader must be at the cost of the death of the Author."[1] This was important to him in a wider political context as well. Denying the authority of the author meant, for Barthes, denying the authority of any person who attempts to govern meaning. This includes lawyers, property owners, and governments who seek to oppress others by controlling their thoughts and actions.

Barthes's main themes of author, reader, and text fit together to prove this conclusion. The unimportance of the author leads to an understanding of texts as an array of discourses and meanings because, without an author, there is no unifying authorial intention to give the text a single meaning. Disregarding the author leads also to a validation of the reader. With authorial intention discounted as the source of a text's meaning, there is now room for the reader to provide this meaning. However, Barthes's notion of the reader was abstract. When he mentions "the reader," he simply means the conceptual space where all possible meanings of a text are contained and understood.

Exploring the Ideas

At the time Barthes wrote "The Death of the Author," the individual genius so lauded by Romanticism* and post-Cartesian* humanism,* had become a firmly capitalistic subject. As an individual who owned and governed their text, the author was linked to capitalist ideas of property. In response to this capitalist appropriation of humanism,

Barthes writes that the literary author in particular is "the epitome and culmination of capitalist ideology, which has attached the greatest importance to the 'person' of the author."[2]

Barthes tackles this conception of subjectivity head-on, contending that authors do not own and control their texts. The text is not the author's own at all, but comprises a wealth of discourses and reader interpretations. Instead, he notes: "Writing is that neutral, composite, oblique space where our subject slips away."[3] Writing is *neutral*: it is not imbued with the individuality of the author's personality. Writing is *composite*: it is not the unified expression of a single authorial personality or discourse, but is a composite of many narratives and layers of meaning. Finally, writing is the site where *our subject slips away*: the text is separate from the individual human person or subjectivity that is the author.

Barthes explicitly formulates his thoughts as a rejection of traditional ideas. He states that the author is a historical construct typical of the emergence of modern subjectivity in the Renaissance.* He writes, "The author is a modern figure insofar as, emerging from the Middle Ages* with English empiricism,* French rationalism* and the personal faith of the Reformation,* it discovered the prestige of the individual, of, as it is more nobly put, the 'human person.'"[4]

The replacement of the author by an entity known as the scriptor was an idea unique to Barthes. Texts are comprised of written words, thus there must be at least some minimal writing process involved in its makeup. Barthes argues that this writing process should not be described as being performed by an author who is of interest in their own right, but as being performed by a neutral, hypothetical entity: the scriptor. Barthes takes care to contrast the author and the scriptor. While the author was traditionally and erroneously thought to be the definite point of origin for the text and the source of its meaning, the scriptor is none of these things, and does not have a personality or biography important to the text. Consider a typist who types up a piece of text almost mechanically without deliberating or intending what to write. The scriptor is akin to the typist. The scriptor cannot limit the meaning of a text. For Barthes, the text is a language inhabited by many meanings. For example, an ambiguous word can have several interpretations. Additionally, a text's future meaning may change as historical and cultural circumstances change.

Language and Expression

Barthes is proposing a new way of understanding texts. As a result, he introduces new vocabulary to describe it. His choice of vocabulary makes these ideas seem unfamiliar at first, but it is clear he has chosen these words for a reason. A key example is the word scriptor, which is a Latin word suggesting someone who simply writes or copies rather than creating or inventing. In the 1968 original French version, this word is *scripteur*. This word sounds out of the ordinary in French as it was not common vocabulary at the time. *Scripteur* also connotes the act of writing as copying-out rather than as creative invention. Barthes's use of words that were not part of common vocabulary of the time alerts readers to the fact that these ideas are new and strange. These words are well chosen because they carry connotations of the writer as someone who simply makes marks on a page without control over the meaning of those marks, instead of as a godlike creative genius.

Barthes facilitates our understanding of this novel and complex idea by using concrete images to describe the scriptor. For instance, he describes the scriptor as a disembodied hand. This is a powerful image of the scriptor's lack of personhood as well as the fact that the scriptor's function is simply to inscribe. The image of the disembodied hand has several other connotations which Barthes may or may not have intended, as they seem to work against his idea of the author. Allusions that may spring to the reader's mind include the disembodied hand that writes words of divine warning in the Biblical tale of Belshazzar's

Feast,* the uncannily alive disembodied hands of Gothic literature, and the practice of automatic writing at séances whereby attendees attempt to achieve a trance-like state and allow their hands to write automatically, disconnected from their brains, so that spirits might speak through them.

NOTES

1   Roland Barthes, "The Death of the Author," in *Image – Music – Text,* trans. Stephen Heath (New York: Hill and Wang, 1977), 148.

2   Roland Barthes, "The Death of the Author," in *Image – Music – Text*, trans. Stephen Heath (New York: Hill and Wang, 1977), 143.

3   Roland Barthes, "The Death of the Author," in *Image – Music – Text*, trans. Stephen Heath (New York: Hill and Wang, 1977), 142.

4   Barthes, "The Death of the Author," 142–3.

MODULE 6
SECONDARY IDEAS

KEY POINTS

- Alongside his main argument, Roland Barthes also examines the role of the critic and the privileging of written language over spoken language.

- His thoughts on readers and critics can be linked to earlier works by writers such as Oscar Wilde.*

- Barthes's idea of the scriptor has Surrealist* connotations.

Other Ideas

The main ideas of Roland Barthes's "The Death of the Author" also bring into play numerous secondary themes. One notable theme is the debate over the precedence of oral and written language; that is, the debate about whether speech or writing is the more important and more ancient form of language. A second key theme is the debate over the status of the critic. These two themes strengthen each other; the rejection of personal speech from written language relates to Barthes's rejection of the personage of the critic.

"The Death of the Author" presents the act of speech as excluded from written language. It is true in a general way that speech ultimately dies with the author while their written words remain, and many individual quirks of an author's speech (such as her or his accent) are not generally represented in writing. However, Barthes's description of the difference between speech and writing evokes a more radical separation of the two. The text inscribed by the scriptor and consumed by the reader has no relation to speech's verbalization. Again, Barthes deploys concrete imagery to express his position within a network of dense philosophical arguments. The scriptor is, he writes, "the hand

> 66 Historically, the reign of the Author has also been
> that of the Critic. 99
> Roland Barthes, "The Death of the Author"

cut off from any voice."[1] Though aiding clarity and simplicity of expression, such imagery may be said to over-simplify the distinction between orality and literacy by suggesting it operates only at a physical, rather than conceptual, level. Orality can be thought of as more than the act of speaking. For example, it can involve whole oral traditions such as folk tales. Literacy can be thought of as more than just the act of writing by hand. It can be related to multiple types of texts, including computer generated texts, texts printed by a printing press, and written texts imagined in the mind.

In his discussion of the reader, Barthes dissociates his ideal of the reader from that of the critic. The importance of the critic as a personage is tied to the importance of the author as such. The critic, in a way which is, to varying degrees, elitist, claims to be the only person who can understand the author of a text, and to possess the one "correct" interpretation of that text. Barthes is arguing here against the elitism of critics who attempt to stop other people from interpreting texts in their own ways. Barthes describes the critic as a kind of oppressive tyrant who seeks "victory" over other readers and enjoys a joint "reign" with the author.[2] The way he expresses his ideas makes it clear that Barthes is vilifying the critic.

Exploring the Ideas

The strong differentiation between speech and language in "The Death of the Author" marks an alteration in Barthes's views. In *Elements of Semiology* (1964), he had argued that language was, by definition, made up of a combination of speech and writing. Here, he critiques "the dichotomic concept of language/speech" (i.e. the idea that speech and language form a dichotomy, two strictly separated phenomena).[3] Barthes was not alone in distinguishing between orality and literacy, a relationship that he explores throughout his body of work and that makes his arguments here part of a historical network of discussion. As with many of the structuralist differentiations between two things, the difference between oral and written language was often modelled by structuralists as hierarchical. In his essay "Plato's Pharmacy," and his later work *The Post Card*, Jacques Derrida critiqued this distinction. Derrida notes that the ability of writing to be codified and used to create a permanent record was often lauded over the ephemeral nature of the spoken word. However, the separation of writing from the human person means that speech could be seen as a more powerful evocation of human presence.

In terms of Barthes's discussion of the critic as a tyrannical figure, it is important to note that Barthes lived in an era when critics were also celebrated personalities and authors in their own right, such as the poet T.S. Eliot.* At the end of the nineteenth century, Oscar Wilde's dialogue "The Critic as Artist" firmly linked the roles of great critic, great artist, and great personality. He describes critics as "worshippers" of "Art as goddess," and that "the highest criticism is a record of one's own soul," giving voice to the same "imaginative passions" as artists.[4] Barthes's attack on the critic was of personal use to academics and students engaged in literary criticism who wished to reflect on this practice.

Overlooked

The surrealist links in "The Death of the Author" are often overlooked in studies of Barthes. Nevertheless, this overlooked aspect of the text aids our understanding of the scriptor.

In "The Death of the Author," Barthes silently links his discussion of the scriptor to a phenomenon known as "automatic writing" by stating that the scriptor is "borne by a pure gesture of inscription."[5]

Automatic writing, also called psychography, was a practice popular in the nineteenth and early to mid-twentieth centuries. It was deployed in both spiritualist* and artistic contexts, and involved mechanically writing whatever the hand was led to write without conscious deliberation. Barthes describes automatic writing early in "The Death of the Author," writing of "the surrealist jolt" which involves "entrusting the hand with the task of writing as quickly as possible what the head itself is unaware of (automatic writing)."[6] This remark is often overlooked in critical studies and appraisals of "The Death of the Author," yet it is an interesting field of study, not least because it illustrates the link between Barthes's thoughts and surrealism.*

Barthes's near contemporary, the surrealist poet André Breton,* sought to create poems that were not governed by a unifying authorial intention. Rather, he used the techniques of automatic writing to create poems that were not consciously directed. Breton announced that he used these techniques throughout his theoretical work on how to write in a surrealist fashion (of which the best known is his 1924 *Manifesto of Surrealism*).

Many thinkers mention Barthes and Breton alongside each other because both men were significant cultural figures of their time. However, comparatively fewer thinkers (among them the present-day literary theorists John Maynard,* who works on literary intention with respect to the Victorian era, and Karl Simms*) successfully draw the link between the surrealist practice of automatic writing and the role of the scriptor in "The Death of the Author."

NOTES

1   Roland Barthes, "The Death of the Author," in *Image – Music – Text*, trans. Stephen Heath (New York: Hill and Wang, 1977), 146.

2   Roland Barthes, "The Death of the Author," in *Image – Music – Text*, trans. Stephen Heath (New York: Hill and Wang, 1977), 147.

3   Roland Barthes, *Elements of Semiology* (New York: Hill and Wang, 1968), p. 34.

4   Oscar Wilde, 'The Critic as Artist', in *The Complete Works of Oscar Wilde* (New York: Harper Collins, first published 1948), 177.

5   Roland Barthes, "The Death of the Author," in *Image – Music – Text*, trans. Stephen Heath (New York: Hill and Wang, 1977), 146.

6   Barthes, "The Death of the Author," 144.

ACHIEVEMENT

KEY POINTS

- Roland Barthes achieves his aim of making an original contribution to ways of thinking about authorship.

- "The Death of the Author" aligned with contemporary critiques of capitalism* and structuralism, but met with resistance from traditionalists.

- "The Death of the Author" is relevant to numerous contexts outside the immediate field of literary analysis.

Assessing the Argument

Overall in "The Death of the Author," Roland Barthes achieves his aim of providing a new way to understand authorship and readership. He asserts at the end of the essay that the origin of a text is no longer important. What is important, he argues, is the direction in which the text is heading. This direction is the reader, or rather, the multiplicity of potential readers and interpretations that could possibly exist, both now and in the future.

Part of Barthes's strategy is to erase authority figures and to replace a single voice with multiplicity. As we have seen, he denies the importance of both authors and critics as authority figures who can determine a text's meaning. Untethered from these single authorities, texts reveal their multiplicity. As Barthes writes, "a text is made of multiple writings, drawn from many cultures, and entering in to mutual relations of dialogue."[1] A reader, or a particular interpretation, can provide a way of focusing the text. But each reader and each interpretation will focus that text in a different way. Looking more closely at the essay, it might be argued that Barthes is very careful

> 66 We are now beginning to let ourselves be fooled no longer by the arrogant antiphrastical recriminations of good society. 99
>
> Roland Barthes, "The Death of the Author"

throughout not to replace the authority figures of the author and critic with the reader as yet another authority figure. He does this by emphasizing the multiplicity of readers and stating that their readings of texts are not definitive. There is no one perfect way to read any given text.

Achievement in Context

Barthes's critique of the importance of the author in "The Death of the Author" was, taken broadly, not new. This was the theme of much mid-twentieth century criticism by writers such as Derrida, Foucault, the New Critics, and the Cambridge School. Moreover, Barthes's discussion of the author as a capitalist owner reflects earlier Marxist literary theory, such as Pierre Macherey's 1966 book *A Theory of Literary Production*. The presence of Marxist theory and arguments critiquing the idea of the author as an authority figure were factors that enabled Barthes to write this text.

Barthes's "The Death of the Author" was an attack on traditional criticism's meticulous contextualization of a text's author, history, and cultural surroundings. As such, it was at times met with a furious reaction from such critics. Traditional critics did not attack Barthes's ideas as expressed in "The Death of the Author" alone. Rather, their criticisms saw Barthes as part of a wider movement. It was New Criticism, structuralism, and post-structuralism as a whole that traditional critics saw as perilously lacking in objectivity. They also saw Barthes as dangerously radical because his idea of the death of the author could be used to resist all forms of traditional authority. We see this when Barthes states in this essay, "We are now beginning to let ourselves be fooled no longer by the arrogant antiphrastical recriminations of good society."[2] Antiphrastical means to use a word in the opposite sense of what it actually means. Thus, Barthes is implying that "good society," along with traditional social morality and customs, condemns ideas that ought to be praised and praises ideas that ought to be condemned. To take a new perspective on the world is to upset this established social order.

Limitations

Though Barthes's main examples are literary ones, the ideas in "The Death of the Author" can be applied to any kind of spoken or written text in numerous fields including literary, political, historical, and legal contexts. Barthes might cause us to ask, for instance, if a politician is really the author of his or her speeches, even though those speeches are considered to have a certain authority because they are spoken by a particular person. In a legal framework, Barthes's ideas might prompt us to revise our ideas of copyright whereby an author owns their text and is given special authority over it because they are the person who wrote it.

It can also be argued that, with the advent of the Internet, Barthes's notion of the death of the author has found another application unforeseen by him in the 1960s. Internet practices such as crowd-sourcing, online phenomena such as community-edited pages, and the widespread copying and dissemination of data between internet users (think of memes or retweeting) mean that every day internet users deal with online texts which are not "owned" by a single, definable author, but are in many ways open to all.

One potential limitation of "The Death of the Author" is that it contains many cultural references which assume readers have certain knowledge they may not actually possess. For example, readers may not be familiar with Balzac's story *Sarrasine,* which Barthes discusses in the opening paragraphs of "The Death of the Author." They may also be unfamiliar with the work of French literary critic and poet Stéphane Mallarmé* who Barthes claims is a significant influence on his idea of the death of the author. To an extent, readers need not possess this prior knowledge, as Barthes explains the relevant aspects of the previous critics and writers upon which he draws. However, in lacking their own knowledge of these critics and writers, readers may have to trust that Barthes's description of them is accurate. This could be a reason for criticizing Barthes. In making us rely on him to tell us what a text means, Barthes is acting precisely like the type of authority figure he is trying to challenge. However, Barthes does not command us not to read Mallarmé. He does not explicitly state that we should take his interpretation for granted. An astute reader will thus go and read Mallarmé for themselves to judge whether or not they agree with Barthes's analysis.

NOTES

1   Roland Barthes, "The Death of the Author," in *Image – Music – Text*, trans. Stephen Heath (New York: Hill and Wang, 1977), 148.

2   Roland Barthes, "The Death of the Author," in *Image – Music – Text*, trans. Stephen Heath (New York: Hill and Wang, 1977), 148.

PLACE IN THE AUTHOR'S WORK

KEY POINTS

- "The Death of the Author" marks Roland Barthes's turn away from structuralism and toward post-structuralism.

- "The Death of the Author" also marks the first definitive moment in Barthes's career when he states that the author is "dead."

- The essay continues to be very significant in academia and the idea of the death of the author has entered firmly into popular culture.

Positioning

"The Death of the Author" is situated at a moment in Roland Barthes's career when he was moving away from structuralist analyses and toward a more post-structuralist way of understanding texts.

Barthes's earlier writings, such as his essay "Introduction to the Structuralist Analysis of Narratives," supported structuralist ways of thinking. In these earlier writings, Barthes attempted to find clear structures in texts based around differences. For example, he focused on the differences between spoken and written language.

In addition, his 1964 book *Elements of Semiology* posits numerous binary oppositions as a foundation for understanding language: "Language and Speech," "Signified and Signifier," "Syntagm and System," and "Denotation and Connotation."[1] The signified is the object a word refers to, while the signifier is the word itself. A syntagma is a system of words. To denote and connote are two slightly different ways of referring to things. A denotation is the literal or primary meaning of a word, while a connotation is the idea or feeling a word

> ❝ Linguistics has recently provided the destruction of the Author with a valuable analytical tool, by showing that the whole of the enunciation is an empty process, functioning perfectly without there being any need for it to be filled with the person of the interlocutors. ❞
>
> Roland Barthes, "The Death of the Author"

invokes in addition to its primary meaning. The use of binary oppositions in constructing systems is fundamental to structuralism. These binaries also tended to become hierarchal; for example, with speech subordinated to language. There are traces of this mode of thought in "The Death of the Author" when Barthes subordinates speech to writing: "Writing is the destruction of every voice."[2]

Barthes's later works exhibit more post-structuralist and deconstructionist leanings. This is because he began to find structuralism limiting in its heavy reliance on the idea of texts as fixed, immoveable systems which could only have one possible interpretation. His 1970 book *S/Z* for instance, emphasizes that there are actually a multitude of potential readings of a text.

Integration

Barthes often re-articulated the concept of the death of the author in later works. For instance, in *The Pleasure of the Text* (1973) he writes: "As an institution the author is dead: his civic status, his biographical person have disappeared." Though Barthes had not announced categorically in his earlier works that he believed in the unimportance of the author to a text's meaning, his body of work prior to 1968 can be read as leading up to this conclusion.

In earlier works, such as *Elements of Semiology* (1964) and the 1966 introduction to *Structural Analysis of Narratives*, he tended to discuss texts as systems of signs and as complex structures, without reference to their authors. This suggests implicitly that he did not believe authors to be important in the processes of understanding and critiquing texts. In particular, his paper for the 1966 Johns Hopkins University seminar on structuralism, "To Write: An Intransitive Verb?" may be seen as an embryonic form of the argument in "The Death of the Author." Here, Barthes limits the role of the "person" to a grammatical category confined within language (the word "I" or "you" for instance), rather than to a real person outside the text.[3] Though a text can be narrated, he argues, the instance of narration does not capture the biography and emotions of the author in the capacity of a person. In *S/Z* (1970), he reiterates his statement from "The Death of the Author" that a text does not have a single meaning but is the product of many different interpretations which "blend and clash" with each other. Barthes's 1953 book *Writing Degree Zero* argues that we should think of texts as neutral, i.e. not shaped by an individual style indicative of authorial personality. This may be seen to anticipate Barthes's concept of the neutral scriptor.

In other earlier works, however, it seems that Barthes applauds texts which bear recognizable traces of individuality. This can be seen in his discussion of stylized writing in his 1953 book *Writing Degree Zero* (*Le degré zéro de l'écriture*). This apparent disunity between Barthes's ideas can be reconciled as his interest in style was arguably more about linguistics than authorial personalities. It might be argued that Barthes was mainly concerned with the unique ways words form patterns in certain literary texts, which can be analyzed without reference to the text's author.

Significance

"The Death of the Author" may be said to stand out from Barthes's earlier writings and mark the energetic introduction of a new idea into his corpus. He began to find the idea that a single fixed concept (such as that of the author) was extremely limiting as it only allowed texts to be interpreted according to the author's presumed intentions. Denying the author this importance enables readers to come up with new and exciting interpretations of texts.

The idea of the death of the author is one of Barthes's most well-known concepts and it continues to have currency. It is still taught in universities and still informs the way scholars write about texts. This idea has also entered firmly into popular culture. Many people have heard the phrase "the death of the author" without realizing it derives from Barthes and without having read Barthes's 1968 essay.

The notion of the death of the author has entered general currency in a somewhat simplified form, almost as a kind of catchphrase. For example, Barthes and the idea of the death of the author appear in cartoons, often with gentle humor. Additionally, obituaries of authors (including Barthes himself) often invoke the phrase "the death of the author." In 1992, the Scottish novelist and poet Gilbert Adair* turned the notion, somewhat satirically, into fiction with his novella *The Death of the Author*. The novella features an author who, though assumed dead by post-Barthesian literary theory, appears alive and kicking as a character in the story. In 2002-03, the Pompidou Centre* in Paris ran an exhibition on Barthes, demonstrating his continued importance to the general thinking public.

NOTES

1   Roland Barthes, *Elements of Semiology* (London: Jonathan Cape, 1967), 14–15, 31–35, 89–93.

2   Roland Barthes, "The Death of the Author," in *Image – Music – Text*, trans. Stephen Heath (New York: Hill and Wang, 1977), 142.

3   Roland Barthes, "To Write: An Intransitive Verb?" in *The Structuralist Controversy: The Languages of Criticism and the Sciences of Man*, ed. Richard Macksey & Eugenio Donato (Baltimore: Johns Hopkins University Press, 1972), 140.

SECTION 3
IMPACT

THE FIRST RESPONSES

KEY POINTS

- Roland Barthes was attacked by Raymond Picard, an academic known for his studies of Jean Racine.*

- In *Criticism and Truth*, Barthes entered into debate with Picard.

- It is still possible to read "The Death of the Author" without looking at it through Picard's lens.

Criticism

Barthes met with positive responses from theorists who were broadly attuned to his way of thinking, such as Julia Kristeva, Jacques Derrida, and Michel Foucault. However, immediately after publishing "The Death of the Author," he met with criticisms from a well-known professor at the time, Raymond Picard.

Picard criticized Barthes for being overly abstract and technical in his vocabulary and thought. Picard argued that this made Barthes's work opaque to the common reader and undercut its freeing potential and its message through inaccessibility. This criticism did not attack Barthes alone but saw him as part of a wider trend of unnecessary abstraction in Continental theory.* The French psychoanalyst Jacques Lacan* and the French philosopher Jean Baudrillard* were just two of Barthes's contemporaries who met with similar accusations from both academic and non-academic circles.

Those academics who attacked Barthes often hailed from prestigious institutions and had built their reputations by publishing books focused on authors' biographies. Picard had made his name through writings on the eminent seventeenth-century French

> **❝** Criticism[:] allotting itself the important task of discovering the Author. **❞**
> Roland Barthes, "The Death of the Author"

dramatist Jean Racine, and Barthes had published essays on Racine which countered Picard's methodology. Picard may have, perhaps rightly, seen Barthes's work as a deliberate attack on his own or perceived as an assault on his professional career. Because so much of Picard's life had been spent on his career and academic reputation, Picard may also have experienced Barthes's work as a personal assault.

Picard argued in his 1964 *New Criticism or New Fraud?* (*Nouvelle Critique ou Nouvelle Imposture?*) that understanding an author's biography is important to anchor a text in historical data and give it some measure of objectivity. Picard's scathing criticism is wide ranging. He attacks what he calls "thematic criticism," which looks at the themes of a text rather than its historical context, and argues that such criticism is deliberately written without concern for clarity and tries to confuse readers.[1] For such critics, an objective or truthful reading of a text was one that focused on historical facts. For Picard, thinkers such as Barthes (whom he mentions explicitly at several points) removed this anchoring, meaning that even the most ridiculous interpretations of a text could be advanced with theoretical credibility. The original French edition of Picard's tract preceded publication of "The Death of the Author" (the English translation did not), yet Picard's attack on Barthes's anti-intentionalism* is indicative of how Barthes's essay was received by his more negative critics.

Responses

Barthes responded to criticisms of his ideas in his 1966 book *Criticism and Truth* (*Critique et Vérité*). This book was not a response to criticisms of "The Death of the Author" specifically, but to the wider criticisms of his thoughts which had been advanced by Raymond Picard in particular. Picard had accused Barthes of failing to recognize that knowledge of a text's author and historical context gives objectivity to a reading of that text. For Picard, the correct and most objective interpretation of a text is one which best fits with what is known about the author's biography, personality, and historical circumstances. According to Picard's theory, when an interpretation of a word or phrase is in doubt, referring to the author's personality and historical context, asking how the author would have intended that phrase, and knowing what it would have meant to people at the time can guide readers toward the correct interpretation. In *Criticism and Truth*, Barthes accuses Picard of being overly pedantic and behind the times. Partly because Picard insists on there being a single correct meaning to a text, and also because he has failed to incorporate new developments in psychoanalysis, literary theory, and cultural studies into his thought.

Criticism and Truth marks the culmination of a critical dialogue between Barthes and Picard. Barthes had originally provoked Picard's anger earlier in the 1960s when he published some critical essays on Picard's area of expertise: Racine. Barthes's critical essays expressed views counter to Picard's traditional biographical and historical mode of criticism. *New Criticism or New Fraud?* was an angry response to these earlier essays by Barthes.

Despite the personal bias and the anger in Picard's criticisms, it is possible to agree with his desire for objectivity in the interpretation of literary texts. Whether or not they use authorial intention as their standard, many readers make judgments about which interpretations of a text are most plausible and which ones yield the "correct" meaning.

Barthes's goal in *Criticism and Truth* was not to revise but to clarify his opinions, which he did with some care. With respect to the accusation that he was not objective enough, Barthes explained that his theory of reading did not aim to be "objective" by providing a single definitively accurate interpretation of a text. However, it was "objective" in the sense of being a logical and scientific approach to literature.[2]

Conflict and Consensus

Challenges to Barthes's New Critical notions contain some persuasive points. The idea of an objective reading of a text is still attractive to many readers who wish to discover the right, or at least the best possible, interpretation of a text. The idea of a single "correct" interpretation of a literary text is valued by those who wish to use texts for propaganda purposes, for example. However, Barthes's critics did little to stem the generally positive reaction to "The Death of the Author," particularly in America and among continental post-structuralists and deconstructionists. In addition, Barthes already absorbs these criticisms into "The Death of the Author" itself, by redefining the key terms of the debate, such as objectivity and authority.

The debate between Barthes and traditional critics such as Picard had little impact on the massive influence of "The Death of the Author." This debate was somewhat of an isolated, personal argument and ran out of steam after a few years. As the notion of the death of the author became more mainstream, thanks to its generally positive reception, other accusations of unnecessary abstraction began likewise to fall somewhat by the wayside. The ascendancy of postmodern literary theory which emphasized the importance of the text over the author meant that, by the end of the 1960s, postmodernists had become the prime target for these accusations rather than Barthes.

NOTES

1   Raymond Picard, *New Criticism or New Fraud* (Washington: Washington University Press, 1969), passim.

2   See Roland Barthes, *Criticism and Truth*, trans. Katrine Pilcher Keuneman (London: Continuum, 2004), 31.

THE EVOLVING DEBATE

KEY POINTS

- "The Death of the Author" was immediately influential among academics and cultural theorists.

- Roland Barthes influenced the school of thought known as structuralist semiology.

- The idea of the death of the author continues to influence debates surrounding authorship today, such as debates about anti-formalism.

Uses and Problems

"The Death of the Author" was, and continues to be, a very influential text. The fact that Roland Barthes's essay coincided with the publication of Derrida and Foucault's works, which also sought to dismantle the status of the author, and with the writings of American deconstructionists such as Geoffrey Hartman,* meant that, by 1968, the notion of the death of the author was powerful and influential.

"The Death of the Author" immediately found an appreciative audience in the United States, where the essay, translated to English by Richard Howard, was first published in a 1967 edition of *Aspen*. *Aspen* was a multimedia journal on the latest developments in the arts, cultural theory, and criticism. The issue in which "The Death of the Author" appeared was called "The Minimalism Issue" and, as was usual with *Aspen*, came in a box format. It contained phonograph recordings by minimalist composers such as John Cage,* creative writing by the conceptual poet Dan Graham,* minimalist cardboard artworks, and essays by other critical thinkers such as Susan Sontag.* As such, Barthes's initial influence spread to a wide variety of academics and

> **❝** The reader is the space on which all the quotations that make up a writing are inscribed without any of them being lost. **❞**
> Roland Barthes, "The Death of the Author"

cultural theorists, as well as anyone interested in theory across the whole spectrum of the humanities.

A growing interest in more radical art forms, such as conceptual poetry* and minimalist art,* as well as interest in structuralist and post-structuralist philosophy, meant Barthes's work was well received by many American intellectuals and aesthetes. "The Death of the Author" was brought to life in an academic context as well. It was presented in embryonic form at an academic seminar on structuralism at Johns Hopkins University in the United States in 1967.

Schools of Thought

"The Death of the Author" has informed almost all key schools of thought in Western philosophy, literary criticism, and textual analysis that deal with questions of authorship. Barthes's work influenced the development of the structuralist, post-structuralist, and deconstructionist movements. Moreover, several schools of thought have also sprung up as a result of Barthes's body of work.

An identifiable present-day school of thought exists around the structuralist and semiotic writings of Barthes and related thinkers. Jonathan Culler's* semiology is heavily influenced by Barthes's structural semiology but also takes into account Barthes's later ideas such as the death of the author. Culler has published several works on semiology as well as on structuralist and deconstructionist literary theory. One of his most famous books is *Structuralist Poetics* (1975). He has also published on Barthes alone, writing *Barthes: A Very Short Introduction* in 1983. Structural semiotics examines texts as systems of signs. These signs are analyzed through their relationships with each other rather than through their relationships with authorial intention or external context.

In the 1980s and 1990s, new debates emerged about the relevance of historical context to the interpretation of literary texts. These debates tended to take Barthes's ideas into account. One critical theorist who sees historical and authorial context as important to literary texts is Stanley Fish.* In his 1991 essay "Intention and Biography," Fish wrote that meaning is determined by a text's context. Fish stated that a fundamental aspect of that context is the author and his or her personal biography, cultural conditions, and historical background. However, Fish also experimented with analyzing texts outside of their context. In his essay "Is There A Text In This Class," he shows a classroom of students a set of random words and tells them that these words are an early modern poem of unknown authorship. The students generate a coherent set of interpretations of the "poem" as if it was written intentionally by an author. The experiment shows that when we interpret texts, we tend to invent an author for them, even if we have no idea who that is.

In Current Scholarship
Barthes's essay continues to inform current scholarship on literary interpretation and authorial intention. Almost all studies of these topics will have taken Barthes's ideas in "The Death of the Author" into account, whether implicitly or explicitly. One example of a recent study is Kaye Mitchell's* 2011 book *Intention and Text: Towards an Intentionality of Literary Form.*[1]

"The Death of the Author" also presents challenges to current scholarship. Anti-formalists are a key intellectual group still challenged by "The Death of the Author." Literary formalism is the theory that only the formal properties of a text (structure, use of tropes, syntax) ought to be considered by interpreters, not the text's context. New

Criticism is thus a type of formalism. Anti-formalists rebut the idea that only the internal formal properties of a text ought to be considered, and often argue that authorial intention is a key source of a text's meaning. In the present day, Stanley Fish is one of the leaders of anti-formalism. Fish argues that postmodern theory, which Barthes influenced, is not all formalist. For Fish, meaning and intention are the same thing. A text can have no meaning unless an element of authorial intention is present, thus authorial intention is always important to interpreting a text. Fish's arguments, like many debates around literary formalism, are intellectually motivated and confined to the specialized field of literary and textual studies (though Fish has also engaged in debate with legal theorist Ronald Dworkin* about the interpretation of legal texts).

NOTES

1   Kaye Mitchell, *Intention and Text: Towards an Intentionality of Literary Form* (New York: Continuum 2011).

MODULE 11
IMPACT AND INFLUENCE TODAY

KEY POINTS

- "The Death of the Author" is now considered a classic work of critical theory.

- Critics working in fields as diverse as linguistics and gender studies continue to be inspired by Roland Barthes's work.

- Barthes's work is challenged by other theorists, including some queer theorists.*

Position

Roland Barthes's "The Death of the Author" has become a striking symbol of literary-theoretical iconoclasm in present-day culture. The phrase is often invoked when any godlike or father-like figure is denied importance to culture. These present-day invocations of the death of the author are indicative of the fact that Barthes's essay has retained its relevance, albeit sometimes in a simplified form.

"The Death of the Author" remains significant to contemporary debate. The continued validation of the author means that Barthes's challenge to their significance remains important. Postmodern theory in particular is founded on the idea of the death of the author.

Lacanian* psychoanalytic theory has contributed to the evolving intellectual environment that has helped to consolidate the popularity of "The Death of the Author." Jacques Lacan posited that subjectivity was both constituted by, and omitted from, language and systems of signification. In the hands of theorists such as Barthes's one-time student, philosopher Julia Kristeva, the similarities

> **❝** The space of writing is to be ranged over not pierced; writing ceaselessly posits meaning ceaselessly to evaporate it, carrying out a systematic exemption of meaning. **❞**
>
> Roland Barthes, "The Death of the Author"

between Barthes's and Lacan's notions of the human subject as a mere function of discourse continue to be explored in the present day.

Barthes's entire corpus has been very influential. Due to the turning-point in his thought, his later writings (especially "The Death of the Author") tend to take precedence over his earlier views on structuralism which he later revoked. His work spans many disciplines, from linguistics to film studies, and his oeuvre has a wide audience. His film "Cher Antonioni" continues to inform film studies and his playful work *A Lover's Discourse* is still given as a gift between lovers.

Interaction

The influence of Barthes's "The Death of the Author" can be traced up to present day postmodernism. Postmodernism tends to seek to destabilize the notion of the author as the originator of a text and its primary source of meaning.

Feminism and queer theory* also continue to display the underlying influence of "The Death of The Author." Thinkers such as gender theorist Judith Butler* question the Romantic, post-Enlightenment, and classic humanist conceptions of the author as an authoritative and paternal subject. These feminist, queer, and gender theorists argue that the subjectivity embodied in this traditional model of the author is definitively male and therefore constitutes a sexist way of thinking. For many feminists, including Butler, the author or authority figure cannot be disregarded as easily as Barthes claims. Feminists often point out that the male authority figure is deeply entrenched in many societies and restricts women's abilities to move further in their careers, to be recognized as equal by the law, and to have their voices heard.

Within the context of a wider critique of capitalism, Marxist literary theory continues to challenge notions of the text as an author's property. In doing so, present-day Marxist thinkers often owe a debt to Barthes's seminal notion of the death of the author. The English literary theorist Terry Eagleton* is perhaps the most famous of such Marxist literary theorists. Eagleton has discussed structuralism and post-structuralism at length and also helped to keep Marxist theory in the spotlight into the present day.

The potential application of Barthes's ideas in the interpretation of legal texts has generated a lively debate. Dworkin demonstrates that legal theory is best understood as being firmly rooted in the attempt to understand the intentions of a legal text's author (e.g. the maker of a statute, the writers of the American Constitution, the author of a will). Some critics, such as Martha Woodmansee* and Peter Jaszi,* argue that the law of intellectual property, which covers issues such as copyright and plagiarism, is overly dominated by the Romantic conception of the literary author as an individual genius, able to own and control the texts he or she has created. They argue that legal theory should consider more recent developments in literary theory which have challenged this romantic ideal, not least Barthes's "The Death of the Author." The reaction from legislators and legal scholars to these kinds of proposals has been practically non-existent; the theory of the death of the author has not been utilized to change the law. This may be because legal scholars rarely look to literary critics for inspiration, preferring instead to refer to works relating strictly to the law.

The Continuing Debate

Psychobiographical literary criticism,* which sees texts as expressions or indications of the author's psychological states, mounts an implicit challenge to "The Death of the Author" and was challenged by Barthes in turn. Proponents of psychobiography rarely take the time to deal with Barthes's arguments in a sustained or serious way. This is perhaps because they often do not come from a literary background but from a psychoanalytic one, and psychoanalysis revolves around other key topics. The motivation of psychobiographical critics when interpreting texts is intellectual but often also professional as many are trained analysts. This school of thought thus incorporates literary, scientific (e.g. cognitive science), and psychoanalytic theory. Norman Holland* is one significant example of such a critic. He challenges the idea of the death of the author by arguing that literary texts, and readers' responses, can be understood as products of neural or psychological stimuli in the mind.

Many feminists have contested the erasure of the body from writing, including the body of the author. Late twentieth and early twenty-first century thinkers such as Hélène Cixous* and Luce Irigaray* have argued that disregarding the body when interpreting texts is a form of oppression. They call for a celebration of the body, particularly the female body and its movements, as a significant source of meaning and a mode of communication. This idea might be said to oppose Barthes's insistence that the individual, biological author is not an authoritative source of meaning.

Some members of existing schools of criticism concerned with gender and sexuality, such as queer theory, are interested in authors' biographies for a different reason. Queer theorists often return to authors who, in less liberal or accepting times, have been mistakenly defined as heterosexual, and attempt to bring to light the homosexual or otherwise queer aspects of these authors' lives and works. Often the agenda of such theorists is to illuminate previously suppressed truths about the homosexual elements of authors' lives, and thus to provide a basis for reinterpreting their works with consideration of queer readings. Barthes's notion of the death of the author could also be deployed today to challenge these critical projects. It is plausible that Barthes, who was increasingly open about his own homosexuality in his published works, would be sympathetic to the concerns of present-day queer theorists. The extent to which Barthes's own writings can be co-opted into a queer agenda is somewhat open to interpretation, not least because his belief in the death of the author would arguably make it ironic to use Barthes's own biography as a source of meaning.

MODULE 12
WHERE NEXT?

KEY POINTS

- The ideas in "The Death of the Author" have the potential to be highly relevant in the future.

- Post-humanism,* linguistics, and psychoanalytic studies are just a few of the fields where Barthes's ideas could inform future work.

- In many ways, "The Death of the Author" remains the model challenge to ideas of the author's authority.

Potential

Several critics, such as American Marxist Frederic Jameson,* have noted that postmodernism and post-structuralism are beginning to be exhausted as theoretical models. They argue that we are currently facing the death of postmodernism and post-structuralism.[1] What this means for "The Death of the Author" is open to interpretation. On one hand, much of the worth of "The Death of the Author" in the present-day stems from its influence on post-structuralism and postmodern theory, and from the ways in which Roland Barthes's ideas have been woven into debates in these theories. This suggests that the demise of postmodernism and post-structuralism will lead to a diminished relevance for Barthes's essay. On the other hand, with the demise of postmodernism, several earlier texts are undergoing a conscious resurrection. Critics are returning to these earlier texts with fresh eyes, aiming to determine their relevance in this new climate. Because it is so seminal, it is likely that "The Death of the Author" will be one of these texts.

> **❝** To give a text an Author is to impose a limit on that text. **❞**
>
> Roland Barthes, "The Death of the Author"

Throughout its history, Barthes's ideas in "The Death of the Author" have shown a peculiar power in remaining influential and relevant, and evolving to provoke new ideas in other thinkers. Though the exact future of "The Death of the Author" is not certain, it is likely that the essay will continue to be relevant both of itself and as a springboard for other ideas.

Aside from his ideas, Barthes himself is increasingly becoming an important figure. In 2009, portions of his journal were published under the title *Journal of Mourning*. These published sections of his journal are largely those which describe his reaction to his mother's death. The book was well received as a tender and touching account of grief by a writer who many found interesting as a person, not simply as a philosopher. The 2002-03 Barthes exhibition at the Pompidou Centre in Paris presented insights into Barthes as a man alongside insights into his philosophical ideas, again attracting interest in both Barthes's life and his thoughts. His postmodern essay *Barthes par Barthes,* which is part-autobiography, part narrative, and part literary-theory was translated by Richard Howard and published as *Roland Barthes By Roland Barthes.*

Future Directions

Several thinkers are demonstrating the influence of Barthes's ideas in a way that also allows for their modification. A present-day example is American literary theorist Jane Gallop,* whose 2011 book *The Deaths of the Author* overtly claims Barthes's essay as an influence. Like Barthes's former student Julia Kristeva, Gallop brings a mixture of other theoretical agendas, such as queer theory and psychoanalysis, to her use of Barthes's ideas. For example, she deploys psychoanalysis to look for traces the supposedly dead author has left in her or his text. She also uses psychoanalytic theories of writing as a way of mourning the dead. It is probable that in the future, "The Death of the Author" may remain central to the intellectual world of critics like Gallop. However, Barthes's ideas will not always be slavishly followed; they will be critiqued and explored in new ways.

Barthes's works are also likely to continue to inform ideas in the field of linguistics. One significant example for the present and future can be found in the works of Jonathan Culler. Culler is a literary theorist whose key interest is in structuralism and semiology. His focus is on explaining how structuralism evolved in the hands of thinkers like Saussure and Barthes, and how it can be applied in literary theory today. As such, Culler's primary interest in Barthes is in his works on semiology and structuralism. Culler is an influential figure whose writings on structuralism tend to be thought of as one of the most comprehensive and definitive guides to the topic in the present day.

Post-humanism is a theory which continues to gain currency and which exhibits many potential resonances with Barthes's idea of the death of the author. Post-humanists question the humanist notion of subjectivity and associated concepts such as consciousness, rationality, and emotion as definitively human. Post-humanists argue that, with the advent of increasingly clever computerized systems, the classic humanist notion of subjectivity being located in the human body is beginning to be challenged.

Summary

"The Death of the Author" is in many ways the model challenge to author-centric modes of literary criticism. In this essay, Barthes articulates a strong argument against the traditional way of reading which sees the author's biography, historical context, personality, and state of mind as the source of a text's meaning. By doing so, he marked a turning point in literary criticism away from this author-centric view. There lies the essay's impact and continuing importance. Additionally, "The Death of the Author" marks a turning point in Barthes's own thoughts as he begins to critique the structuralism he embraced in his earlier works. For these reasons, students will benefit from reading "The Death of the Author."

On a practical level, despite the far-reaching influence and longevity of Barthes's ideas, readers' appetites for knowledge of an author's personality and biography continue to inform their appreciation of literary texts. Readers still flock to author readings and book signings. Biographies of famous authors and other cultural personages continue to be bought in great abundance. Barthes continues to provide us with a way of thinking critically about these cultural practices and the assumptions about authorship that lie behind them.

NOTES

1   Frederic Jameson. *Postmodernism, or the Cultural Logic of Late Capitalism* (London: Verso, 1991).

GLOSSARY

GLOSSARY OF TERMS

Anti-intentionalism: the dismissal of intentionalism which states that a text's meaning is to be found in authorial intention.

Aspen: a multimedia magazine published by Phyllis Johnson between 1965 and 1971.

Autonomy: making and carrying out decisions for and by oneself.

Belshazzar's Feast: A Biblical story in which Belshazzar drinks from vessels that had been looted in the destruction of First Temple. During the feast, a disembodied hand appears and writes a message from God on the wall.

Cambridge School: centering on figures like F. R. Leavis, William Empson, Q. D. Leavis and T. S. Eliot, the Cambridge School argued that knowledge of an author's biography or the historical context was not significant in helping us understand the text. Rather, we should look at the ambiguities in the text, the relation of the words to each other, and the literary devices used.

Capitalism: economic model based on principles of private ownership, and thus emphasizing the individual person as a property owner.

Capitalist: a person who invests in trade and industry for profit according to the principles of capitalism.

The Cold War (1947-91): A period of political tension and hostility between the Union of Soviet Socialist Republics (USSR) and American-led Western nations.

Conceptual Poetry: experimental poetry which uses conceptual restraints and often strict rules.

Continental Theory (or Continental Philosophy): intellectual traditions of Continental Europe during the nineteenth and twentieth centuries.

Deconstruction: a literary and philosophical movement that criticized the idea that there are any stable axioms and hierarchies. One of the most famous deconstructionists is Jacques Derrida.

Empiricism: the system of natural philosophy based on experiments in the observable world.

The Enlightenment: a term for the seventeenth and eighteenth century movement in Western thought toward more scientific ways of seeing the world. The Enlightenment is often seen as the time in which traditional religious and superstitious ideas were challenged by scientific thought. The post-Enlightenment period, which many critics believe has extended to the present-day, is deeply influenced by the scientific movement of the Enlightenment.

Freudian: the psychoanalytical teachings of Sigmund Freud.*

Heteronormative: the idea that heterosexuality is the norm and that it ought to be sustained as the norm.

The Highway Code: a set of information, advice, guides, and rules for road users in the United Kingdom.

Humanism/Humanist: a school of thought which focuses on human rationality as a means of inquiry rather than on the divine.

Iconoclastic: literally, "destroying icons." Something iconoclastic breaks the mold or challenges ideas that had been thought of as undeniably true or sacred.

The Intentional Fallacy: a term used in twentieth-century literary criticism to describe the problem of judging a work of art based on assumptions about the intent or purpose of the artist.

Intentionalism: the theory that a literary work should be judged by the author's intentions.

Intertextual: the relationships between several texts, whereby one text influences another or several texts influence each other. This term first appeared in literary theory in the 1970s.

Johns Hopkins: a university in Baltimore, founded in 1876.

Lacanian: pertaining to the ideas and theories of French psychoanalyst Jacques Lacan.

Lycée: a state funded secondary school in France.

Manteia: French magazine in which "The Death of the Author" had its French debut in 1968.

Marxist: a person who believes in the socialist teachings of Karl Marx.*

Middle Ages: a term used to describe the period after the classical era and before the Renaissance.

Minimalist Art: visual art that uses minimal shape and color.

NATO: also known as the North Atlantic Treaty Organization, NATO is a military alliance between several North American and European countries.

New Criticism: an American school of criticism which flourished in the mid-twentieth century. It sought to interpret literary texts as autonomous entities, understood apart from their historical context, their author, and their readers.

Oedipus Complex: Freud's theory that a young male child harbors a suppressed wish to marry his mother and kill his father as the legendary Oedipus did.

Pompidou Centre: a cultural centre in Paris, France.

Post-Cartesian: a philosophical and psychological position, anticipatory of poststructuralist theory, in which it is assumed that mind, body and language interact, rather than being separate, as Descartes proposed.

Post-Enlightenment: the period after the Enlightenment era. (see The Enlightenment)

Post-Humanism: the idea or philosophy that humanity can be transformed or eliminated by technological or evolutionary advances.

Post-structuralism/Post-structuralists: a theoretical movement that came after, and critiqued, structuralism. Post-structuralists challenged the structuralist ideal of a coherent, stable system.

Psychoanalysis: a therapeutic method, originated by Sigmund Freud, for treating mental disorders. This method investigates the interaction of conscious and unconscious elements in the patient's mind. It brings repressed fears and conflicts into the conscious mind by using techniques such as dream interpretation and free association. Also: a system of psychological theory associated with this method. (*OED*)

Psychobiographical Literary Criticism: a school that deploys psychological theory in an attempt to understand and analyze the author, and hence to interpret texts.

Queer Theorists: academics engaged in the study of queer theory.

Queer Theory: theory relating to texts and cultural practices that do not conform to heterosexual norms.

Rationalism: a system of philosophy based around human rationality.

Reformation: the move from Catholicism to Protestantism in the Renaissance era.

Renaissance: literally meaning 'rebirth', the Renaissance was characterized by the rebirth of classical knowledge.

Romantic: pertaining to Romanticism.

Romanticism: a movement in the arts that flourished during the early to mid-nineteenth century. It emphasized the importance of individual genius and helped to foster the cult of the individual.

Semiology: the study of both linguistic and non-linguistic signs.

Spiritualism/Spiritualist: the belief that one can communicate with the souls of the deceased.

Structuralism: a critical movement. Structuralists argued that we can understand phenomena in a range of disciplines, from anthropology to linguistics, as part of a wider system.

Surrealism/Surrealist: artistic or literary works featuring realistic depictions of highly fantastical and dreamlike forms or events.

USSR: the Union of Soviet Socialist Republics was a socialist state which existed from 1922 to 1991. The USSR was governed by the Russian Communist Party and included modern-day Ukraine, Georgia, Latvia, Lithuania, and Belarus, among other countries.

PEOPLE MENTIONED IN THE TEXT

Gilbert Adair (1944-2011) was a Scottish novelist, poet, film critic, and journalist. He was critically acclaimed for his translation of the postmodern novel *A Void* by Georges Perec in which the letter *e* is not used.

Honoré de Balzac (1799-1850) was writer born in Tours, France. He wrote novels, short stories, and plays which centered on keen observations of French society, particularly the rise and fall of Emperor Napoleon Bonaparte.

Jean Baudrillard (1929-2007) was a cultural theorist who is best known for his writings about popular culture. For example, he discussed fashion and consumer culture as systems of signs.

Monroe Beardsley (1915-85) was a philosopher of aesthetics and New Critic.

Charles Beaudelaire (1821-1867) was a French poet and art critic known for his original style of prose-poetry. He is credited with coining the term "modernity".

André Breton (1896-1966) was a French writer and poet known for founding Surrealism.

Judith Butler (b. 1956) is an American philosopher and gender theorist. She teaches at the University of California, Berkeley and is best known for her books *Gender Trouble: Feminism and the Subversion of Identity* and *Bodies That Matter: On the Discursive Limits of Sex*.

John Cage (1912–1992) was an American composer and music theorist. He was a pioneer of indeterminacy in music, electroacoustic music, and non-standard use of musical instruments.

Hélène Cixous (b. 1937) is a French feminist philosopher and creative writer. Her work focuses on the themes of language and the body.

Jonathan Culler (b. 1944) is a professor of English at Cornell University. He is famous for his work on semiology.

Jacques Derrida (1930–2004) was a French-Algerian philosopher and the founder of deconstruction.

Ronald Dworkin (1931–2013) was an American legal theorist and political philosopher. Dworkin was interested in how we interpret legal texts, as evidenced in his book *Law's Empire.*

Terry Eagleton (b. 1943) is a British Marxist literary critic.

T. S. Eliot (1888–1965) was a US-born British poet and literary critic.

William Empson (1906–1984) was an English literary critic.

Stanley Fish (b. 1938) is an American literary theorist. He is famous for his works on interpretation and readers' responses.

Michel Foucault (1926–1984) was a French philosopher known for works such as *The Archaeology of Knowledge* and *Discipline and Punish.*

Sigmund Freud (1856-39) was an Austrian neurologist who progressed from studying the neural makeup of worms to founding psychoanalysis.

Jane Gallop (b. 1952) is an American literary theorist. Her works focus on ideas of meaning, reading, and intentionality.

Charles de Gaulle (1890-1970): was a French general and politician. He was the leader of Free France during World War II and president of France from 1958-1969.

Dan Graham (b. 1942) is an American artist, writer, and curator. His work often multimedia and focuses on cultural phenomena.

Geoffrey Hartman (1929-2016) was an American literary theorist whose work focused on deconstruction.

Stephen Heath is Professor of English and French Literature at Jesus College, Cambridge. He was a colleague of Barthes and in 1977 translated "The Death of the Author" into English.

Norman Holland (b. 1927) is an American literary theorist who often focuses on psychoanalysis. Holland has written works on many literary texts, including Shakespeare's plays.

Richard Howard (b. 1929) is a North American poet and translator.

Luce Irigaray (b. 1932) is a Belgian feminist psychoanalyst and philosopher. She controversially refuted many male-centered axioms of philosophy and psychoanalysis such as the Freudian idea of penis envy.

Frederic Jameson (b. 1934) is a North American Marxist literary critic.

Peter Jaszi is an American specialist on copyright law.

Julia Kristeva (b.1941) is a Bulgarian-French philosopher and psychoanalyst. A former student of Barthes, she is known for works such as *Black Sun*.

Jacques Lacan (1901-81) was an influential psychoanalyst known for his theories of language and signification.

F. R. Leavis (1895-1978) was an English literary critic.

Claude Lévi-Strauss (1908-2009) was a French anthropologist who helped develop the discipline of structural anthropology.

Pierre Machery (b. 1939) was a French literary critic based at the University of Lille. Machery's critical works have a Marxist framework.

Stéphane Mallarmé (1842-1898) was a French symbolist poet. His work inspired Cubism, Futurism, Dadaism, and Surrealism.

John Maynard is a professor of English at New York University whose work includes the topic of intentionality in literature.

Karl Marx (1818-1883) was a German political philosopher and economist whose theories were radically socialist.

Kaye Mitchell is a senior lecturer at the University of Manchester in the School of Arts, Languages and Cultures.

Raymond Picard (1917-75) was a French literary critic and Sorbonne professor. Picard was famous for his works on the French playwright Racine. He was opposed to the New Critical movement.

Georges Poulet (1901-91) was a Belgian literary critic. Though he was often described as a New Critic, Poulet rejected both formalism and the idea that we can discover a text's meaning by plumbing the depths of its author's mind. Instead, he described texts as having a consciousness all of their own which stems from the author.

Marcel Proust (1871-1922) was a novelist and literary critic born in Auteil in the suburbs of Paris. He is best known for his monumental novel in seven books called *In Search of Lost Time*.

Jean Racine (1639-1699) was a French dramatist. Along with Moliere and Corneille he is considered one of the three great playwrights of seventeenth century France.

Ferdinand de Saussure (1857-1913) was a Swiss linguist. He was a great influence on Barthes's early work.

Karl Simms is an academic in Liverpool, United Kingdom, who works on the intersection between literature, philosophy, and psychoanalysis.

Susan Sontag (1933-2004) was an American writer, filmmaker, teacher, and political activist. She is known for her works *On Photography, Against Interpretation,* and *In America*.

Vincent Van Gogh (1853-1890) was a Dutch post-Impressionist painter.

Oscar Wilde (1854–1900) was an Irish playwright and author of several prose works. He moved to London early in his career.

William Kurtz Wimsatt Jr. (1907–75) was a literary theorist and New Critic. He worked together with Monroe Beardsley.

Martha Woodmansee (b. 1944) is an American professor of English and expert in the intersection of law and literature.

WORKS CITED

WORKS CITED

Barthes, Roland. *Criticism and Truth*. Translated by Katrine Pilcher Keuneman. London: Continuum, 2004.

"The Death of the Author," In *Image-Music-Text*. Translated by Stephen Heath. New York: Hill and Wang, 1978.

Elements of Semiology. Translated by Annette Lavers and Colin Smith. New York: Hill and Wang, 1977.

The Pleasure of the Text. Translated by Richard Miller. New York: Hill and Wang, 1975.

Roland Barthes. New York: Farrar, Straus, and Giroux, 1977.

"To Write: An Intransitive Verb?" in *The Structuralist Controversy: The Languages of Criticism and the Sciences of Man*, ed. Richard Macksey & Eugenio Donato. Baltimore: Johns Hopkins University Press, 1972.

Culler, Jonathan. *Structuralist Poetics: Structuralism, Linguistics and the Study of Literature*. London: Routledge, 2002.

Derrida, Jacques. *Of Grammatology*. Translated by Gayatri Spivak. Chicago: Chicago University Press, 1967.

The Truth in Painting. Translated by Geoff Bennington and Ian McLeod. Chicago: Chicago University Press, 1978.

Writing and Difference. Translated by Alan Bass. London: Routledge & Kegan Paul, 1978.

Fish, Stanley. *Is There a Text In This Class? The Authority of Interpretive Communities*. Cambridge MA: Harvard University Press, 1982.

Foucault, Michel. "What is an Author?" In *Language, Counter-Memory, Practice*. New York: Cornell University Press, 1969.

Jameson, Frederic. *Postmodernism, or the Cultural Logic of Late Capitalism*. London: Verso, 1991.

Macherey, Pierre. *A Theory of Literary Production*. Translated by Geoffrey Wall. London: Routledge, 2006.

Maynard, John. *Literary Intention*. New York: Broadview Press, 2009.

Mitchell, Kaye. *Intention and Text: Towards an Intentionality of Literary Form*. New York: Continuum, 2011.

Picard, Raymond. *New Criticism or New Fraud*. Washington: Washington University Press, 1969.

Wilde, Oscar. *The Complete Works of Oscar Wilde*. Introduced by Merlin Holland. New York: Harper Collins, 1948.

THE MACAT LIBRARY
BY DISCIPLINE

AFRICANA STUDIES

Chinua Achebe's *An Image of Africa: Racism in Conrad's Heart of Darkness*
W. E. B. Du Bois's *The Souls of Black Folk*
Zora Neale Huston's *Characteristics of Negro Expression*
Martin Luther King Jr's *Why We Can't Wait*
Toni Morrison's *Playing in the Dark: Whiteness in the American Literary Imagination*

ANTHROPOLOGY

Arjun Appadurai's *Modernity at Large: Cultural Dimensions of Globalisation*
Philippe Ariès's *Centuries of Childhood*
Franz Boas's *Race, Language and Culture*
Kim Chan & Renée Mauborgne's *Blue Ocean Strategy*
Jared Diamond's *Guns, Germs & Steel: the Fate of Human Societies*
Jared Diamond's *Collapse: How Societies Choose to Fail or Survive*
E. E. Evans-Pritchard's *Witchcraft, Oracles and Magic Among the Azande*
James Ferguson's *The Anti-Politics Machine*
Clifford Geertz's *The Interpretation of Cultures*
David Graeber's *Debt: the First 5000 Years*
Karen Ho's *Liquidated: An Ethnography of Wall Street*
Geert Hofstede's *Culture's Consequences: Comparing Values, Behaviors, Institutes and Organizations across Nations*
Claude Lévi-Strauss's *Structural Anthropology*
Jay Macleod's *Ain't No Makin' It: Aspirations and Attainment in a Low-Income Neighborhood*
Saba Mahmood's *The Politics of Piety: The Islamic Revival and the Feminist Subject*
Marcel Mauss's *The Gift*

BUSINESS

Jean Lave & Etienne Wenger's *Situated Learning*
Theodore Levitt's *Marketing Myopia*
Burton G. Malkiel's *A Random Walk Down Wall Street*
Douglas McGregor's *The Human Side of Enterprise*
Michael Porter's *Competitive Strategy: Creating and Sustaining Superior Performance*
John Kotter's *Leading Change*
C. K. Prahalad & Gary Hamel's *The Core Competence of the Corporation*

CRIMINOLOGY

Michelle Alexander's *The New Jim Crow: Mass Incarceration in the Age of Colorblindness*
Michael R. Gottfredson & Travis Hirschi's *A General Theory of Crime*
Richard Herrnstein & Charles A. Murray's *The Bell Curve: Intelligence and Class Structure in American Life*
Elizabeth Loftus's *Eyewitness Testimony*
Jay Macleod's *Ain't No Makin' It: Aspirations and Attainment in a Low-Income Neighborhood*
Philip Zimbardo's *The Lucifer Effect*

ECONOMICS

Janet Abu-Lughod's *Before European Hegemony*
Ha-Joon Chang's *Kicking Away the Ladder*
David Brion Davis's *The Problem of Slavery in the Age of Revolution*
Milton Friedman's *The Role of Monetary Policy*
Milton Friedman's *Capitalism and Freedom*
David Graeber's *Debt: the First 5000 Years*
Friedrich Hayek's *The Road to Serfdom*
Karen Ho's *Liquidated: An Ethnography of Wall Street*

The Macat Library By Discipline

John Maynard Keynes's *The General Theory of Employment, Interest and Money*
Charles P. Kindleberger's *Manias, Panics and Crashes*
Robert Lucas's *Why Doesn't Capital Flow from Rich to Poor Countries?*
Burton G. Malkiel's *A Random Walk Down Wall Street*
Thomas Robert Malthus's *An Essay on the Principle of Population*
Karl Marx's *Capital*
Thomas Piketty's *Capital in the Twenty-First Century*
Amartya Sen's *Development as Freedom*
Adam Smith's *The Wealth of Nations*
Nassim Nicholas Taleb's *The Black Swan: The Impact of the Highly Improbable*
Amos Tversky's & Daniel Kahneman's *Judgment under Uncertainty: Heuristics and Biases*
Mahbub Ul Haq's *Reflections on Human Development*
Max Weber's *The Protestant Ethic and the Spirit of Capitalism*

FEMINISM AND GENDER STUDIES

Judith Butler's *Gender Trouble*
Simone De Beauvoir's *The Second Sex*
Michel Foucault's *History of Sexuality*
Betty Friedan's *The Feminine Mystique*
Saba Mahmood's *The Politics of Piety: The Islamic Revival and the Feminist Subject*
Joan Wallach Scott's *Gender and the Politics of History*
Mary Wollstonecraft's *A Vindication of the Rights of Woman*
Virginia Woolf's *A Room of One's Own*

GEOGRAPHY

The Brundtland Report's *Our Common Future*
Rachel Carson's *Silent Spring*
Charles Darwin's *On the Origin of Species*
James Ferguson's *The Anti-Politics Machine*
Jane Jacobs's *The Death and Life of Great American Cities*
James Lovelock's *Gaia: A New Look at Life on Earth*
Amartya Sen's *Development as Freedom*
Mathis Wackernagel & William Rees's *Our Ecological Footprint*

HISTORY

Janet Abu-Lughod's *Before European Hegemony*
Benedict Anderson's *Imagined Communities*
Bernard Bailyn's *The Ideological Origins of the American Revolution*
Hanna Batatu's *The Old Social Classes And The Revolutionary Movements Of Iraq*
Christopher Browning's *Ordinary Men: Reserve Police Batallion 101 and the Final Solution in Poland*
Edmund Burke's *Reflections on the Revolution in France*
William Cronon's *Nature's Metropolis: Chicago And The Great West*
Alfred W. Crosby's *The Columbian Exchange*
Hamid Dabashi's *Iran: A People Interrupted*
David Brion Davis's *The Problem of Slavery in the Age of Revolution*
Nathalie Zemon Davis's *The Return of Martin Guerre*
Jared Diamond's *Guns, Germs & Steel: the Fate of Human Societies*
Frank Dikotter's *Mao's Great Famine*
John W Dower's *War Without Mercy: Race And Power In The Pacific War*
W. E. B. Du Bois's *The Souls of Black Folk*
Richard J. Evans's *In Defence of History*
Lucien Febvre's *The Problem of Unbelief in the 16th Century*
Sheila Fitzpatrick's *Everyday Stalinism*

Eric Foner's *Reconstruction: America's Unfinished Revolution, 1863-1877*
Michel Foucault's *Discipline and Punish*
Michel Foucault's *History of Sexuality*
Francis Fukuyama's *The End of History and the Last Man*
John Lewis Gaddis's *We Now Know: Rethinking Cold War History*
Ernest Gellner's *Nations and Nationalism*
Eugene Genovese's *Roll, Jordan, Roll: The World the Slaves Made*
Carlo Ginzburg's *The Night Battles*
Daniel Goldhagen's *Hitler's Willing Executioners*
Jack Goldstone's *Revolution and Rebellion in the Early Modern World*
Antonio Gramsci's *The Prison Notebooks*
Alexander Hamilton, John Jay & James Madison's *The Federalist Papers*
Christopher Hill's *The World Turned Upside Down*
Carole Hillenbrand's *The Crusades: Islamic Perspectives*
Thomas Hobbes's *Leviathan*
Eric Hobsbawm's *The Age Of Revolution*
John A. Hobson's *Imperialism: A Study*
Albert Hourani's *History of the Arab Peoples*
Samuel P. Huntington's *The Clash of Civilizations and the Remaking of World Order*
C. L. R. James's *The Black Jacobins*
Tony Judt's *Postwar: A History of Europe Since 1945*
Ernst Kantorowicz's *The King's Two Bodies: A Study in Medieval Political Theology*
Paul Kennedy's *The Rise and Fall of the Great Powers*
Ian Kershaw's *The "Hitler Myth": Image and Reality in the Third Reich*
John Maynard Keynes's *The General Theory of Employment, Interest and Money*
Charles P. Kindleberger's *Manias, Panics and Crashes*
Martin Luther King Jr's *Why We Can't Wait*
Henry Kissinger's *World Order: Reflections on the Character of Nations and the Course of History*
Thomas Kuhn's *The Structure of Scientific Revolutions*
Georges Lefebvre's *The Coming of the French Revolution*
John Locke's *Two Treatises of Government*
Niccolò Machiavelli's *The Prince*
Thomas Robert Malthus's *An Essay on the Principle of Population*
Mahmood Mamdani's *Citizen and Subject: Contemporary Africa And The Legacy Of Late Colonialism*
Karl Marx's *Capital*
Stanley Milgram's *Obedience to Authority*
John Stuart Mill's *On Liberty*
Thomas Paine's *Common Sense*
Thomas Paine's *Rights of Man*
Geoffrey Parker's *Global Crisis: War, Climate Change and Catastrophe in the Seventeenth Century*
Jonathan Riley-Smith's *The First Crusade and the Idea of Crusading*
Jean-Jacques Rousseau's *The Social Contract*
Joan Wallach Scott's *Gender and the Politics of History*
Theda Skocpol's *States and Social Revolutions*
Adam Smith's *The Wealth of Nations*
Timothy Snyder's *Bloodlands: Europe Between Hitler and Stalin*
Sun Tzu's *The Art of War*
Keith Thomas's *Religion and the Decline of Magic*
Thucydides's *The History of the Peloponnesian War*
Frederick Jackson Turner's *The Significance of the Frontier in American History*
Odd Arne Westad's *The Global Cold War: Third World Interventions And The Making Of Our Times*

The Macat Library By Discipline

LITERATURE

Chinua Achebe's *An Image of Africa: Racism in Conrad's Heart of Darkness*
Roland Barthes's *Mythologies*
Homi K. Bhabha's *The Location of Culture*
Judith Butler's *Gender Trouble*
Simone De Beauvoir's *The Second Sex*
Ferdinand De Saussure's *Course in General Linguistics*
T. S. Eliot's *The Sacred Wood: Essays on Poetry and Criticism*
Zora Neale Huston's *Characteristics of Negro Expression*
Toni Morrison's *Playing in the Dark: Whiteness in the American Literary Imagination*
Edward Said's *Orientalism*
Gayatri Chakravorty Spivak's *Can the Subaltern Speak?*
Mary Wollstonecraft's *A Vindication of the Rights of Women*
Virginia Woolf's *A Room of One's Own*

PHILOSOPHY

Elizabeth Anscombe's *Modern Moral Philosophy*
Hannah Arendt's *The Human Condition*
Aristotle's *Metaphysics*
Aristotle's *Nicomachean Ethics*
Edmund Gettier's *Is Justified True Belief Knowledge?*
Georg Wilhelm Friedrich Hegel's *Phenomenology of Spirit*
David Hume's *Dialogues Concerning Natural Religion*
David Hume's *The Enquiry for Human Understanding*
Immanuel Kant's *Religion within the Boundaries of Mere Reason*
Immanuel Kant's *Critique of Pure Reason*
Søren Kierkegaard's *The Sickness Unto Death*
Søren Kierkegaard's *Fear and Trembling*
C. S. Lewis's *The Abolition of Man*
Alasdair MacIntyre's *After Virtue*
Marcus Aurelius's *Meditations*
Friedrich Nietzsche's *On the Genealogy of Morality*
Friedrich Nietzsche's *Beyond Good and Evil*
Plato's *Republic*
Plato's *Symposium*
Jean-Jacques Rousseau's *The Social Contract*
Gilbert Ryle's *The Concept of Mind*
Baruch Spinoza's *Ethics*
Sun Tzu's *The Art of War*
Ludwig Wittgenstein's *Philosophical Investigations*

POLITICS

Benedict Anderson's *Imagined Communities*
Aristotle's *Politics*
Bernard Bailyn's *The Ideological Origins of the American Revolution*
Edmund Burke's *Reflections on the Revolution in France*
John C. Calhoun's *A Disquisition on Government*
Ha-Joon Chang's *Kicking Away the Ladder*
Hamid Dabashi's *Iran: A People Interrupted*
Hamid Dabashi's *Theology of Discontent: The Ideological Foundation of the Islamic Revolution in Iran*
Robert Dahl's *Democracy and its Critics*
Robert Dahl's *Who Governs?*
David Brion Davis's *The Problem of Slavery in the Age of Revolution*

Alexis De Tocqueville's *Democracy in America*
James Ferguson's *The Anti-Politics Machine*
Frank Dikotter's *Mao's Great Famine*
Sheila Fitzpatrick's *Everyday Stalinism*
Eric Foner's *Reconstruction: America's Unfinished Revolution, 1863-1877*
Milton Friedman's *Capitalism and Freedom*
Francis Fukuyama's *The End of History and the Last Man*
John Lewis Gaddis's *We Now Know: Rethinking Cold War History*
Ernest Gellner's *Nations and Nationalism*
David Graeber's *Debt: the First 5000 Years*
Antonio Gramsci's *The Prison Notebooks*
Alexander Hamilton, John Jay & James Madison's *The Federalist Papers*
Friedrich Hayek's *The Road to Serfdom*
Christopher Hill's *The World Turned Upside Down*
Thomas Hobbes's *Leviathan*
John A. Hobson's *Imperialism: A Study*
Samuel P. Huntington's *The Clash of Civilizations and the Remaking of World Order*
Tony Judt's *Postwar: A History of Europe Since 1945*
David C. Kang's *China Rising: Peace, Power and Order in East Asia*
Paul Kennedy's *The Rise and Fall of Great Powers*
Robert Keohane's *After Hegemony*
Martin Luther King Jr.'s *Why We Can't Wait*
Henry Kissinger's *World Order: Reflections on the Character of Nations and the Course of History*
John Locke's *Two Treatises of Government*
Niccolò Machiavelli's *The Prince*
Thomas Robert Malthus's *An Essay on the Principle of Population*
Mahmood Mamdani's *Citizen and Subject: Contemporary Africa And The Legacy Of Late Colonialism*
Karl Marx's *Capital*
John Stuart Mill's *On Liberty*
John Stuart Mill's *Utilitarianism*
Hans Morgenthau's *Politics Among Nations*
Thomas Paine's *Common Sense*
Thomas Paine's *Rights of Man*
Thomas Piketty's *Capital in the Twenty-First Century*
Robert D. Putman's *Bowling Alone*
John Rawls's *Theory of Justice*
Jean-Jacques Rousseau's *The Social Contract*
Theda Skocpol's *States and Social Revolutions*
Adam Smith's *The Wealth of Nations*
Sun Tzu's *The Art of War*
Henry David Thoreau's *Civil Disobedience*
Thucydides's *The History of the Peloponnesian War*
Kenneth Waltz's *Theory of International Politics*
Max Weber's *Politics as a Vocation*
Odd Arne Westad's *The Global Cold War: Third World Interventions And The Making Of Our Times*

POSTCOLONIAL STUDIES

Roland Barthes's *Mythologies*
Frantz Fanon's *Black Skin, White Masks*
Homi K. Bhabha's *The Location of Culture*
Gustavo Gutiérrez's *A Theology of Liberation*
Edward Said's *Orientalism*
Gayatri Chakravorty Spivak's *Can the Subaltern Speak?*

The Macat Library By Discipline

PSYCHOLOGY

Gordon Allport's *The Nature of Prejudice*
Alan Baddeley & Graham Hitch's *Aggression: A Social Learning Analysis*
Albert Bandura's *Aggression: A Social Learning Analysis*
Leon Festinger's *A Theory of Cognitive Dissonance*
Sigmund Freud's *The Interpretation of Dreams*
Betty Friedan's *The Feminine Mystique*
Michael R. Gottfredson & Travis Hirschi's *A General Theory of Crime*
Eric Hoffer's *The True Believer: Thoughts on the Nature of Mass Movements*
William James's *Principles of Psychology*
Elizabeth Loftus's *Eyewitness Testimony*
A. H. Maslow's *A Theory of Human Motivation*
Stanley Milgram's *Obedience to Authority*
Steven Pinker's *The Better Angels of Our Nature*
Oliver Sacks's *The Man Who Mistook His Wife For a Hat*
Richard Thaler & Cass Sunstein's *Nudge: Improving Decisions About Health, Wealth and Happiness*
Amos Tversky's *Judgment under Uncertainty: Heuristics and Biases*
Philip Zimbardo's *The Lucifer Effect*

SCIENCE

Rachel Carson's *Silent Spring*
William Cronon's *Nature's Metropolis: Chicago And The Great West*
Alfred W. Crosby's *The Columbian Exchange*
Charles Darwin's *On the Origin of Species*
Richard Dawkin's *The Selfish Gene*
Thomas Kuhn's *The Structure of Scientific Revolutions*
Geoffrey Parker's *Global Crisis: War, Climate Change and Catastrophe in the Seventeenth Century*
Mathis Wackernagel & William Rees's *Our Ecological Footprint*

SOCIOLOGY

Michelle Alexander's *The New Jim Crow: Mass Incarceration in the Age of Colorblindness*
Gordon Allport's *The Nature of Prejudice*
Albert Bandura's *Aggression: A Social Learning Analysis*
Hanna Batatu's *The Old Social Classes And The Revolutionary Movements Of Iraq*
Ha-Joon Chang's *Kicking Away the Ladder*
W. E. B. Du Bois's *The Souls of Black Folk*
Émile Durkheim's *On Suicide*
Frantz Fanon's *Black Skin, White Masks*
Frantz Fanon's *The Wretched of the Earth*
Eric Foner's *Reconstruction: America's Unfinished Revolution, 1863-1877*
Eugene Genovese's *Roll, Jordan, Roll: The World the Slaves Made*
Jack Goldstone's *Revolution and Rebellion in the Early Modern World*
Antonio Gramsci's *The Prison Notebooks*
Richard Herrnstein & Charles A Murray's *The Bell Curve: Intelligence and Class Structure in American Life*
Eric Hoffer's *The True Believer: Thoughts on the Nature of Mass Movements*
Jane Jacobs's *The Death and Life of Great American Cities*
Robert Lucas's *Why Doesn't Capital Flow from Rich to Poor Countries?*
Jay Macleod's *Ain't No Makin' It: Aspirations and Attainment in a Low Income Neighborhood*
Elaine May's *Homeward Bound: American Families in the Cold War Era*
Douglas McGregor's *The Human Side of Enterprise*
C. Wright Mills's *The Sociological Imagination*

Thomas Piketty's *Capital in the Twenty-First Century*
Robert D. Putman's *Bowling Alone*
David Riesman's *The Lonely Crowd: A Study of the Changing American Character*
Edward Said's *Orientalism*
Joan Wallach Scott's *Gender and the Politics of History*
Theda Skocpol's *States and Social Revolutions*
Max Weber's *The Protestant Ethic and the Spirit of Capitalism*

THEOLOGY

Augustine's *Confessions*
Benedict's *Rule of St Benedict*
Gustavo Gutiérrez's *A Theology of Liberation*
Carole Hillenbrand's *The Crusades: Islamic Perspectives*
David Hume's *Dialogues Concerning Natural Religion*
Immanuel Kant's *Religion within the Boundaries of Mere Reason*
Ernst Kantorowicz's *The King's Two Bodies: A Study in Medieval Political Theology*
Søren Kierkegaard's *The Sickness Unto Death*
C. S. Lewis's *The Abolition of Man*
Saba Mahmood's *The Politics of Piety: The Islamic Revival and the Feminist Subject*
Baruch Spinoza's *Ethics*
Keith Thomas's *Religion and the Decline of Magic*

Macat Disciplines

Access the greatest ideas and thinkers across entire disciplines, including

Postcolonial Studies

Roland Barthes's *Mythologies*
Frantz Fanon's *Black Skin, White Masks*
Homi K. Bhabha's *The Location of Culture*
Gustavo Gutiérrez's *A Theology of Liberation*
Edward Said's *Orientalism*
Gayatri Chakravorty Spivak's *Can the Subaltern Speak?*

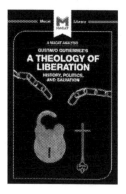
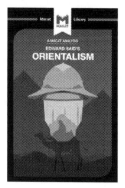

Macat analyses are available from all good bookshops and libraries.

Access hundreds of analyses through one, multimedia tool.

Join free for one month **library.macat.com**

Macat Disciplines

Access the greatest ideas and thinkers across entire disciplines, including

GLOBALIZATION

Arjun Appadurai's, *Modernity at Large: Cultural Dimensions of Globalisation*

James Ferguson's, *The Anti-Politics Machine*

Geert Hofstede's, *Culture's Consequences*

Amartya Sen's, *Development as Freedom*

Macat Pairs

Analyse historical and modern issues from opposite sides of an argument. Pairs include:

HOW TO RUN AN ECONOMY

John Maynard Keynes's
The General Theory OF Employment, Interest and Money

Classical economics suggests that market economies are self-correcting in times of recession or depression, and tend toward full employment and output. But English economist John Maynard Keynes disagrees.

In his ground-breaking 1936 study *The General Theory*, Keynes argues that traditional economics has misunderstood the causes of unemployment. Employment is not determined by the price of labor; it is directly linked to demand. Keynes believes market economies are by nature unstable, and so require government intervention. Spurred on by the social catastrophe of the Great Depression of the 1930s, he sets out to revolutionize the way the world thinks

Milton Friedman's
The Role of Monetary Policy

Friedman's 1968 paper changed the course of economic theory. In just 17 pages, he demolished existing theory and outlined an effective alternate monetary policy designed to secure 'high employment, stable prices and rapid growth.'

Friedman demonstrated that monetary policy plays a vital role in broader economic stability and argued that economists got their monetary policy wrong in the 1950s and 1960s by misunderstanding the relationship between inflation and unemployment. Previous generations of economists had believed that governments could permanently decrease unemployment by permitting inflation—and vice versa. Friedman's most original contribution was to show that this supposed trade-off is an illusion that only works in the short term.

Macat analyses are available from all good bookshops and libraries.

Access hundreds of analyses through one, multimedia tool.
Join free for one month **library.macat.com**

Macat Disciplines

Access the greatest ideas and thinkers across entire disciplines, including

THE FUTURE OF DEMOCRACY

Robert A. Dahl's, *Democracy and Its Critics*
Robert A. Dahl's, *Who Governs?*
Alexis De Toqueville's, *Democracy in America*
Niccolò Machiavelli's, *The Prince*
John Stuart Mill's, *On Liberty*
Robert D. Putnam's, *Bowling Alone*
Jean-Jacques Rousseau's, *The Social Contract*
Henry David Thoreau's, *Civil Disobedience*

Macat analyses are available from all good bookshops and libraries.

Access hundreds of analyses through one, multimedia tool.
Join free for one month **library.macat.com**